Christin

ELEGANT
knotted
JEWELRY

Becky Meverden

kp

CINCINNATI, OHIO
mycraftivity.com
connect. create. explore.

about the author

Becky Meverden, who calls herself "The Constant Crafter," has spent more than twenty years in the craft industry. She is the author of nine books, and her designs have been featured in numerous magazines. She appeared regularly on HGTV's *The Carol Duvall Show*. Becky moved to Suwon, South Korea, in the summer of 2007, where she learned maedeup (Korean knotting). You can read about her adventures in South Korea on the Internet at http://meverden.blogspot.com.

media

www.fwmedia.com.

13 12 11 10 09   5 4 3 2 1

DISTRIBUTED IN CANADA BY FRASER DIRECT
100 Armstrong Avenue
Georgetown, ON, Canada L7G 5S4
Tel: (905) 877-4411

DISTRIBUTED IN THE U.K. AND EUROPE BY DAVID & CHARLES
Brunel House, Newton Abbot, Devon, TQ12 4PU, England
Tel: (+44) 1626 323200, Fax: (+44) 1626 323319
Email: postmaster@davidandcharles.co.uk

DISTRIBUTED IN AUSTRALIA BY CAPRICORN LINK
P.O. Box 704, S. Windsor NSW, 2756 Australia
Tel: (02) 4577-3555

Library of Congress Cataloging-in-Publication Data
Meverden, Becky.
  Elegant knotted jewelry / Becky Meverden. -- 1st ed.
    p. cm.
  Includes index.
  ISBN-13: 978-0-89689-818-9 (pbk. : alk. paper)
  ISBN-10: 0-89689-818-0 (pbk. : alk. paper)
  1. Macramé--Patterns. 2. Macramé--Korea. 3. Knots and splices--Korea. 4. Beadwork--Korea. 5. Jewelry making. I. Title.
  TT840.M33M38 2009
  746.42'2--dc22

                    2009010587

Edited by Jennifer Claydon
Production edited by Liz Casler
Designed by Rachael Smith
Production coordinated by Matt Wagner
Styling by Lauren Emmerling
Photography by Becky Meverden, Curt Meverden, Richard Deliantoni

Metric Conversion Chart

To convert	to	multiply by
Inches	Centimeters	2.54
Centimeters	Inches	0.4
Feet	Centimeters	30.5
Centimeters	Feet	0.03
Yards	Meters	0.9
Meters	Yards	1.1

acknowledgments

My thanks to the people of South Korea for their generosity and acceptance of a couple of *miguks* (Korean for "Americans").

To my Korean maedeup teacher, Kim Su-Mi, for her patience and encouragement in overcoming the language barrier to instruct me.

My thanks also to Mr. Chae Chang-Uk, my Korean yoga buddy, who was there if we needed anything during our stay in Suwon, South Korea.

To Carol Duvall, the Queen of Crafts, for her friendship and support to myself and the entire craft world.

To my book editor, Liz Casler from Krause Publications, for all her diligence and care to make this book what I envisioned it to be.

To Candy Wiza, acquisitions editor at Krause Publications, for believing in me and maedeup from the very beginning.

To my incredible support system: Linda Wyszynski, Holly Dare, Lynn Heppner, Renee Nelson, Lisa Sisterman, Steve Harrington, Kim Ji-Hyun (Jennifer) and Park Lang-Kyu (Jeff).

To Trish, Rita and Jacki at Donatelli's in White Bear Lake, Minnesota. We did miss our favorite Italian restaurant while living in Korea.

To Tammy Browning-Smith for her legal expertise on my behalf.

To my family, who supported us in our decision to move to South Korea:

Our children: Laura, Brent (our son-in-law) and our precious grandson, Noah; Luke, who took care of the house in our absence.

Our parents: Michael and Vivian Seyller; Charles and Alice Meverden.

My sisters: Wendy (Go Packers) Johnson and Heidi (Go Bears) Passmore.

Nephews and nieces: Cole, Hayley, Colin and Madison.

The biggest thank-you is to my husband, Curt, who never complained when dinner wasn't on the table, the house wasn't clean and laundry was still in the basket. Thank you for taking the step-by-step pictures for the book. The book would have never come to fruition without your support.

I would also like to thank the following companies who provided products used in this book: Beacon Adhesives, Inc., Fire Mountain Gems and Beads, Kreinik, Rings & Things, the Satin Cord Store and Swarovski North America Limited.

dedication

This book is dedicated to my Seoul sisters: Lee Soo-Kyoung (Hannah) and Hwang Hye-Ok (Hellena). From translating maedeup classes to exploring South Korea with us, they always greeted us with big smiles. They were always happy to help, whether it was providing translation for a Korean dental visit or sightseeing when our U.S. family members visited. This book is a reality because of them. They will forever be in our hearts.

Kamsamnida (thank you), my friends,
Becky

April is cherry blossom time in South Korea. It is one of the most beautiful things I have ever seen. Koreans love to get out and enjoy the outdoors with their families. I take time to appreciate the beauty around me now, and I have South Korea to thank for that. The day after I took this picture it rained and the blossoms were gone.

foreword
by carol duvall

My friend Becky Meverden is an amazer. That's not a word that's in the dictionary, but it should be. From the first time Becky walked into our studios where we taped *The Carol Duvall Show*, Becky amazed us. She amazed and delighted us all with her wonderful tiny polymer clay creatures, and she amazed and impressed us as well with her ability to so quickly adapt to the demands and restrictions of demonstrating them on television. The viewers loved her, and she quickly became a show regular.

But television wasn't enough. Along the way she wrote books about her miniature polymer clay menagerie, and when there seemed to be a sudden interest in beads and beading among crafters, Becky started beading too.

Then out of the blue came the move to Korea! Becky's husband was sent to South Korea on a business assignment, and the two had no sooner settled into their apartment in Suwon when Becky began to search out the local crafts. Having absolutely no knowledge of the language, not a clue about the ways of this part of the world, and with no interpreter nearby, the search was not easy, but Becky persevered. Before long she had enrolled in a maedeup (knot-tying) class. Once again she amazed those around her by mastering some of the complicated and involved knotting techniques that are treasured as an art in Korea. The teacher and store owners who initially had been concerned that the language barrier would make it too difficult for the American to learn this respected Asian craft were soon proud of their determined student as she moved from beginner knots through intermediate to advanced.

But of course there's more. Before returning to the States, Becky wrote this book to share her newfound knowledge with her fellow American crafters. Becky provides clearly written explanations and helpful hints, plus a few suggestions about patience and practice. There are excellent explanatory step-by-step photographs taken by her husband, Curt, that show you how the knots are made. You'll find a wonderful variety of projects including earrings, necklaces and bracelets. There's something for every female on your gift list, including yourself.

But most exciting of all is the opportunity to learn something new. Maedeup may be an honored, old-world craft to the Koreans, but I dare say it will be brand-new to the American crafting scene, and you'll be the one introducing it to your friends. How fun is that?

Enjoy!

Carol Duvall

Carol Duvall
The Carol Duvall Show

Necklaces

introduction

Journey to South Korea

In the summer of 2007, my husband was given the opportunity through his work to relocate to South Korea for a few years. It was always a dream of his to have this experience, and I felt it was a good time to do it. The hardest part was saying goodbye to our family and friends. We arrived in Korea in July of 2007 to begin what would turn out to be a life-changing adventure.

The first thing I noticed when we arrived at the Incheon International Airport in South Korea happened to be in the airport souvenir shops. Everywhere I looked, I saw items such as cell phone charms, key chains and compacts accessorized with intricate knots. It was beautiful and, being "The Constant Crafter," I instantly knew the craft I wanted to learn. I researched Korean knotting on the Internet and that is how I discovered *maedeup* (pronounced mae-doop).

Through the Korean agency hired by my husband's company to provide help to foreigners moving to South Korea, I met the two girls who were to become my friends for life, Hellena and Hannah. I told Hellena that I wanted to learn maedeup. She found a maedeup shop in Seoul that was willing to teach an American whose Korean was nonexistent.

I soon found myself spending Saturdays in Seoul at maedeup class with Hellena and Hannah. Each week began with learning a new maedeup and concluded with a project that incorporated that maedeup. We made cell phone charms, jewelry and wall hangings. The five-hour classes flew by. Maedeup became a comforting friend to me. It helped me to relax and just be creative.

I had no idea that South Korea was so beautiful, from its glorious mountains to magnificent palaces. There are not many places in the world where you can walk right out of your house and hike a mountain. It is also a shopper's dream, with Namdaemun Market, Dongdaemun Market and Insadong, just to name a few key spots. Korean food was also incredible and delicious no matter where we chose to dine. We became very attached to *kimchi*, which is fermented cabbage with a variety of seasonings. There are more than one hundred different varieties, and it is a staple at every Korean meal.

Until our move, I was also completely unaware of the talent of the Korean people. There are too many Korean crafts to name, but I found myself collecting as many of them as I could carry at any given time. I hope that this book will bring a little bit of Korea into your life. During our stay in South Korea, the Korean government had commercials running with the saying "Korea Sparkling!" I could not have said it better myself.

history

It is said that maedeup takes heart and soul to create. It is a demanding craft that requires concentration and discipline. Maedeup enables you to create art using nothing but cording, an awl and your fingers. Koreans use maedeup as a way to send wishes to loved ones: long life, wealth, protection and fertility. Korean maedeup has thirty-eight basic knots. They are symmetrical from side to side and identical from front to back. There are four steps to creating maedeup: dyeing the thread, making the cord (*dahoe*), constructing the maedeup and making the tassel (*sul*). Koreans believe maedeup keeps the mind sharp due to some of the complexity in creating the knots. Also, it is wonderful for dexterity. Your fingers are in constant motion when creating maedeup. Tightening the maedeup builds strength. It is a fantastic workout for your fingers.

Knot making dates back to the Stone Age when hunters used knots to make belts to carry their tools and weapons. The origins of maedeup can be found only in paintings, drawings, statues and ceramics. The maedeup disintegrated with time, leaving no trace. A wall painting found in Goguryeo, North Korea, dated 357 AD, is the oldest record of maedeup.

Maedeup is found on Buddhist statues and in written records from the Unified Silla Kingdom period (668–935). But maedeup became prominent in Korea during the Joseon period (1392–1910) when it was used in both royal court and daily life. It had many uses: in men's and women's clothing, jewelry and pouches, and for decorating fans, chopsticks, swords, banners and musical instruments. For example, a wife would construct a maedeup for her husband to wear as a good-luck charm or as protection as he went off to war. Maedeup could also be found decorating Buddhist monasteries and temples. It was used in many homes as a decoration.

Maedeup was passed down from mother to daughter, generation to generation, with almost no written record. It almost disappeared in the late nineteenth century when royal courts disappeared. In 1968, South Korea's Cultural Heritage Administration named maedeup the 22nd Important Intangible Cultural Property in order to preserve this ancient art form.

Korean masters of maedeup, such as Kim Hee-jin, have worked diligently to preserve maedeup for future generations. She founded the Kim Hee-jin Traditional Craft Institute in 1973 and began teaching classes in maedeup. In 1979, along with her students, she founded the Korea Maedeup Research Institute.

Hellena, Hannah (my Korean girlfriends) and I took weekly maedeup classes on Saturdays and tried to meet at a coffee shop in Seoul during the week to practice. This night I was sitting across from Hellena and thinking that I didn't ever want to forget that moment. My camera came out and I captured it forever.

MATERIALS & TECHNIQUES

This chapter introduces you to the materials and techniques needed to begin maedeup. For materials, you'll need cording and an awl. Neither is expensive, and what you can create with them is priceless. The cording comes in many colors and sizes. My favorite size to work with is 1.5mm cording. In addition to your two primary materials, pendants and beads are fun to collect and incorporate into maedeup.

You do not need a lot of space for maedeup supplies. While living in South Korea, I bought a floor-to-ceiling garment rack at my local retail chain store. At the same store I also found large hooks that fit the railings (and they were on sale). This is what I continue to use to store my cording. The cording is displayed by diameter and then by color. It's wonderful to be able to see everything I have clearly laid out with easy access.

The most important part of this book is the *Maedeup Techniques* section. Each maedeup is broken down into carefully detailed steps with plenty of photos. The secret to learning maedeup is lots of practice. I try to do some maedeup every day for the simple joy it brings to me. I hope it will do the same for you.

materials

Cording

When I took maedeup classes in Seoul, South Korea, we used Korean cording, which is still my favorite. Korean cording and Chinese cording are made out of braided cotton. The important thing to remember when starting out is the larger the diameter of the cording, the easier the maedeup is to construct. Another important element is the stiffness of the cording. Maedeup is easier to construct on stiffer cording. Many different types of materials work well for maedeup in addition to Korean cording: Chinese cording, satin cording (rattail), hemp and suede, just to name a few. The best way to determine if cording is suitable for maedeup is to test it out with a few maedeup and see what it looks like and how it is to work with.

Awl

You use an awl to tighten the maedeup. The type of awl you need is called a scratch awl and is used in leather crafting. They can be found in some craft stores and on the Internet. An ice pick would also work, although it would be rather large and possibly awkward to handle.

Scissors

Embroidery scissors work best because they are small and very sharp. You need to cut the cording cleanly and sometimes cut very near the maedeup. You want small scissors that won't accidentally cut into your maedeup.

Loop Turner

A loop turner is generally used to turn sewn tubes of fabric right-side out. It is made of metal with a latch on one end. When used for maedeup, the cording is placed into the latch, and the latch is closed and drawn through the maedeup, leaving the maedeup undisturbed. Loop turners can be found in fabric stores and on the Internet. You can also substitute a blunt needle such as a cross-stitch needle.

Beads and Pendants

The sky is the limit for the beads and pendants you can incorporate into your maedeup jewelry. The most important consideration is the diameter of the center hole of the item. The cording has to be able to pass through the hole, and depending on your design, two cords may have to pass through. Pendants make an elegant focal point for maedeup jewelry.

Findings

Findings are a simple, classic way to embellish your maedeup jewelry. Bead shops and craft stores carry a wide range of choices. Fold-over crimps along with a toggle clasp are a great way to finish your necklace or bracelet.

Adhesives

You can use any type of glue in maedeup. Whenever you cut the cording, you need to apply glue to the ends to keep them from fraying and to keep the maedeup from coming apart. Cyanoacrylate glues such as Super Glue or Zap-A-Gap work well to adhere findings to the cording. I always use a toothpick to apply the glue for more control.

Ruler

You need a ruler for measuring between the maedeup and for measuring the length of the jewelry project.

tips for getting started

The only way to master maedeup is through practice. The more you practice, the more you will improve. I can't tell you how many times my Korean maedeup instructor undid my work because I had made a mistake or it wasn't up to her standards.

When you first begin to learn maedeup, use two different colored cords. This will make it easier to see the path of the maedeup. When working with two cords, knot them together before you begin the maedeup. You can switch over to one color of cording when you have mastered the maedeup.

The cording may twist as you work. Gently untwist the cord and continue working. If the cord remains twisted, the maedeup will be misshapen. The finished maedeup piece may also have some twisted cording. To untwist, simply hold the twisted section over a steaming kettle or pot of boiling water to loosen the cording so you can straighten the section out.

Apply glue to the cord ends to keep them from fraying. Beads are also easier to thread when the cord ends are glued.

Calculating the Cordage

It would be very upsetting to get halfway through a project and find out you don't have enough cording. When beginning your own jewelry designs, start by creating a sketch, using symbols for the maedeup (see the example sketch, at right, for the necklace on page 17).

Use the chart on page 17 as a guide to calculate the amount of cording needed for the necklace. First, decide what diameter cording you will use. For this sample, I used 2mm cording. Next, total each type of maedeup used: 6 yeonbong, 18 dorae, 8 hapjong and 2 garakji. Then multiply the total number of each maedeup by the coordinating lengths in the chart:

6 × 2¼" = 13½" (6 × 5.7cm = 34.2cm)
18 × 1⅜" = 24¾" (18 × 3.5cm = 63cm)
8 × ⅞" = 7" (8 × 2.2cm = 17.8cm)
2 × 4¾" = 9½" (2 × 12.1cm = 24.2cm).

The total cording needed for the maedeup alone is 54¼" (137.8cm).

Next, total the non-maedeup part of the necklace: ½" + 1" + 3½" + ½" = 5.5" × 2 (both sides of the necklace) + ½" (focal bead length) for a total of 11½" (1.3cm + 2.5cm + 8.9cm + 1.3cm = 14cm × 2 + 1.3cm = 29.3cm). Added to the maedeup total, this gives you a total of 66¾" (167.1cm). I always add an extra 18 inches to 2 feet to be on the safe side. This necklace uses two lengths of cording, so for extra insurance add 36" (18" for each cord). The total amount of cording needed for this necklace is 102¾".

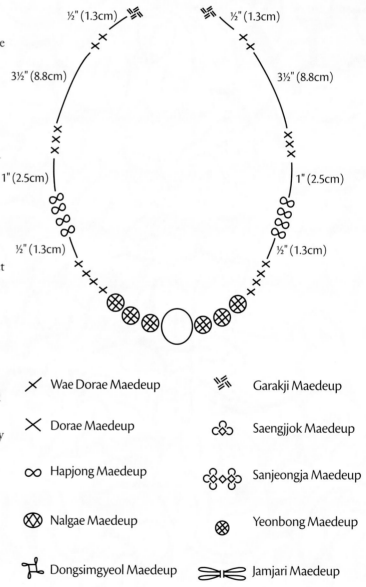

Symbol	Name	Symbol	Name
✗	Wae Dorae Maedeup	𝍂	Garakji Maedeup
✕	Dorae Maedeup	⬡	Saengjjok Maedeup
∞	Hapjong Maedeup	⬡	Sanjeongja Maedeup
⊗	Nalgae Maedeup	⊛	Yeonbong Maedeup
Dongsimgyeol Maedeup		Jamjari Maedeup	

Tightening

The final step to completing your jewelry is tightening the maedeup. Using an awl, begin tightening at the start of the maedeup, not at the end. Follow the cord around the maedeup, keeping the shape of the maedeup as you work. The final maedeup should be symmetrical and identical, front to back and side to side. It is also important to concentrate during tightening. I have gotten distracted and forgotten the direction I was going and had to start all over again.

Maedeup	1mm	1.2 or 1.5mm	2mm
Wae Dorae	⅞" (2.2cm)	1 ⁷⁄₁₆" (3.7cm)	1 ⅞" (4.8cm)
Dorae	⅞" (2.2cm)	1 ⅛" (2.9cm)	1 ⅜" (3.5cm)
Hapjong	⁷⁄₁₆" (1.1cm)	¹³⁄₁₆" (2.1cm)	⅞" (2.2cm)
Nalgae	⅞" (2.2cm)	1½" (3.8cm)	2" (5.1cm)
Garakji (1 cord)	7½" (19.1cm)	7 ⅞" (20cm)	10" (25.4cm)
Garakji (2 cord)	3" (7.6cm)	4 ⅛" (10.5cm)	4¾" (12.1cm)
Saengjjok (1 cord)	2¼" (5.7cm)	4½" (11.4cm)	5" (12.7cm)
Saengjjok (2 cord)	1" (2.5cm)	2" (5.1cm)	2 ⅛" (5.4cm)
Sanjeongja	3" (7.6cm)	5" (12.7cm)	6¼" (15.9cm)
Yeonbong (1 cord)	2¼" (5.7cm)	3¾" (9.5cm)	4 ⅝" (11.7cm)
Yeonbong (2 cord)	1" (2.5cm)	1½" (3.8cm)	2¼" (5.7cm)

maedeup techniques

Dorae (doh-ray)

The dorae maedeup is also known as the double connection knot and looks like an X. This is the most widely used maedeup. It is commonly used to anchor other maedeup. I love this maedeup and how it looks, especially when used consecutively. It is my favorite because it was the very first maedeup I learned. My maedeup teacher told me that to get a baby to shake his head, Koreans say, "dorae, dorae," and the baby will shake his head side to side.

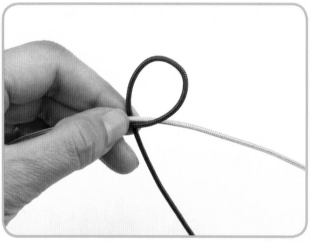

1 Using two cords, use your right fingers to loop the purple cord around the pink cord. (Remember, when creating maedeup with two cords, tie the cords together at one end before beginning). Anchor the loop with your left thumb and index finger.

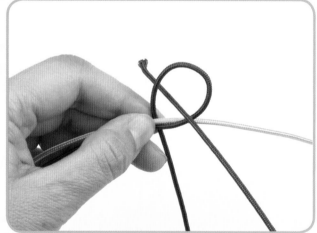

2 Thread the purple cord all the way through the loop. Anchor the base of the loop using your left thumb and index finger.

3 Use your right thumb and index finger to pull the purple cord from the base of the loop. This will make the loop move from the top to the bottom of the cording. Anchor the loop with your left thumb and index finger.

4 Take the pink cord with your right fingers and loop it around the purple cord to create a second loop. Anchor the pink loop to the left of the base of the purple loop using your left index finger and thumb.

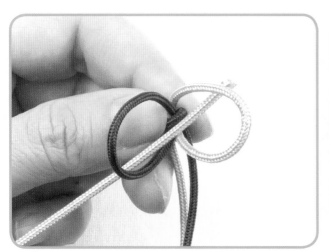

5 Take the pink cord with your right fingers and thread it through both the purple and pink loops. Use your left thumb and index finger to anchor the base of the loops. Gently pull the purple cord with your right fingers from the right side until the maedeup is tightened and then repeat with the pink cord.

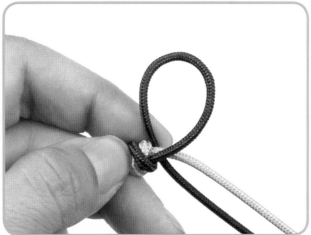

6 (Optional) When making consecutive dorae maedeup, begin the new dorae close to the previous dorae. This will help keep the maedeup uniform and straight.

Wae Dorae (way doh-ray)

This maedeup looks like the dorae maedeup, but it uses only one cord. It's important to keep a tight grip on the cording when you are sliding it off your finger so it doesn't become uncrossed. It will create an X when completed. I use it a lot when I need to anchor a bead on a cord.

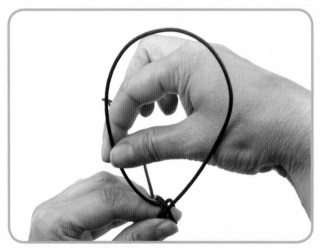

1 Using one cord, wrap the cord around your left index finger to create an X.

2 Continue wrapping the cord around your index finger, crossing over the X.

3 Use your left thumb and index finger to anchor the cord. Gently slip the cord to the tip of your index finger. Thread the cord under the X from left to right using your right thumb and index finger.

4 Pull both ends of the cord to tighten.

Hapjong (hop-jahng)

The hapjong maedeup is also known as the snake knot. It represents happiness together and resembles fingers intertwined in prayer. There are a few Korean proverbs regarding snakes: "You're adding legs to a snake" means you are making too much out of something, and "If you sing at night, a snake will appear" means to be quiet, which hearkens back to times when windows were open at night and walls were thin.

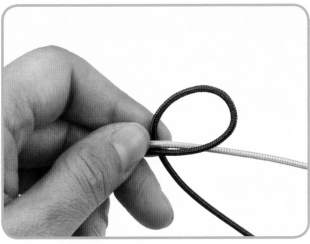

1 Using two cords, use your right hand to loop the purple cord around the pink. Use your left thumb and index finger to hold the loop in place.

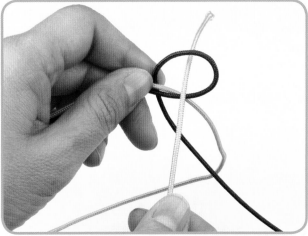

2 With your right hand, reach under the purple cord to grasp the pink cord. Thread the pink cord through the purple loop from front to back. Hold the pink cord tightly at the base of the loop using your left thumb and index finger. Use your right hand to pull the purple cord tight. Also tighten the pink cord.

3 (Optional) When making consecutive hapjong maedeup, make the loops close to the previous hapjong maedeup. This will keep the hapjong maedeup uniform and straight.

Nalgae (nal-gay)

This knot is also known as the wing, the Chinese double coin and the Josephine knot. It resembles two overlapping Chinese coins with a square hole in the center. It lies flat and is not meant to be tied too tightly.

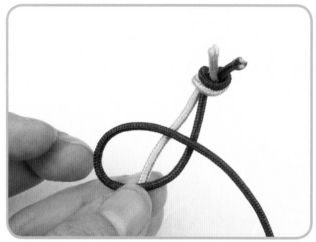

1 With two cords, use your right hand to loop and center the purple cord over the pink cord.

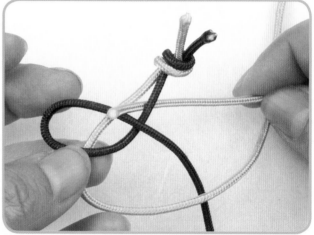

2 Use your right hand to thread the pink cord over the purple cord and up through the top center loop.

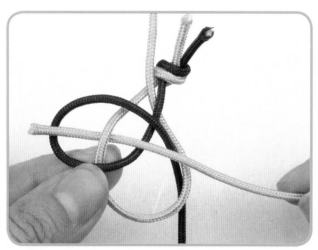

3 Continue by threading the pink cord over the purple loop and under the pink loop.

4 Tighten the loops to complete. The center two lines will be going toward the left.

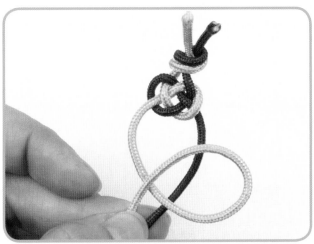

5 (Optional: Steps 5–8 describe how to make a maedeup that is a mirror image of the first. You must complete all 8 steps to create consecutive nalgae.) To make the second nalgae maedeup, begin by using your right hand to loop and center the pink cord over the purple cord.

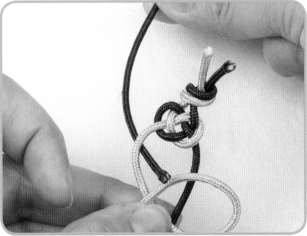

6 Use your right hand to loop the purple cord to the left of and over the bottom end of the pink cord and thread it behind and up through the top center loop.

7 Continue by threading the purple cord over the pink loop and under the purple cord.

8 Tighten the loops to complete. The center two lines will be going toward the right. Repeat all 8 steps to continue making alternating nalgae maedeup.

Dongsimgyeol (dohng-sheem-gyeol)

This knot is also known as the one mind and the good-luck knot. Brides commonly wore it as a symbol of loyalty and good luck. The dongsimgyeol maedeup signified a wish that the couple would be of the same temperament and that there would be harmony between the two.

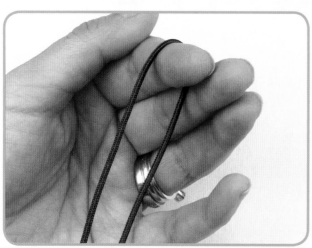

1 Decide how long you want the loops on the finished dongsimgyeol maedeup. For this example we will use 2" (5cm). Loop the cord around your left index finger.

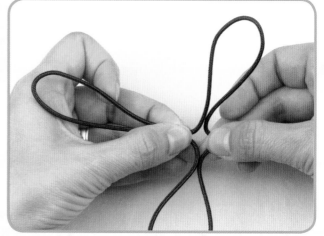

2 Measure 2" (5cm) from the top of the loop and pinch with your left middle finger and thumb. From where your fingers are pinching, double the first measurement, which would be 4" (10cm), and pinch this spot with your right middle finger and thumb. Bring your right index finger and thumb to your left index finger and thumb, which will create two additional loops. From here on, the loop opposite the cord ends shall be considered the center loop, the loop counterclockwise of the center loop shall be the left loop, and the last loop shall be the right loop.

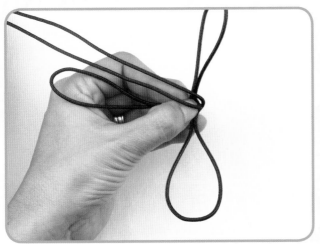 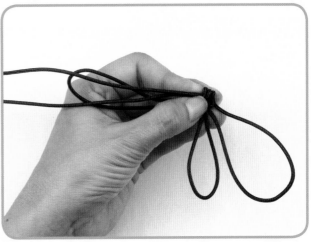

3 You will be working counterclockwise to construct the maedeup. Transfer the cording to your left fingers without losing the loops. Hold the center with your left index and middle fingers along with your left thumb. Take the cord ends and fold them over to the right side of the center loop.

4 Take the right loop (the next loop to the right of the cord ends) and fold it over the center to the opposite side, to the left of the left loop.

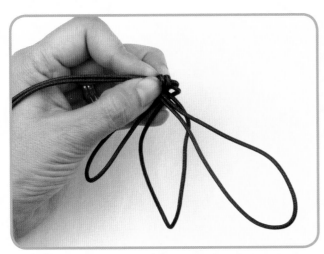 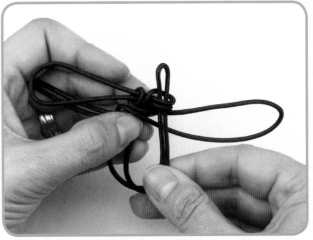

5 Take the center loop (the next loop continuing counterclockwise) and fold it over the center to the opposite side, to the right of the left loop (the final loop).

6 Use your right fingers to loosen the base loops of the first loop that was made with the cord ends. Take the left loop (the last loop) and loop it through these base loops. Use your fingers to pull all the loops at the same time to tighten. The side without the corner loops is the side you will be working on.

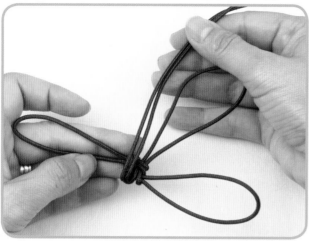

7 The loop now opposite the cord ends becomes the center loop, the loop to its left the left loop, and the last loop the right loop. Going clockwise, fold the cord ends over the center to the left side of the center loop.

8 Take the left loop (the next loop to the left of the cord ends) and fold it over the center to the opposite side, above the right loop.

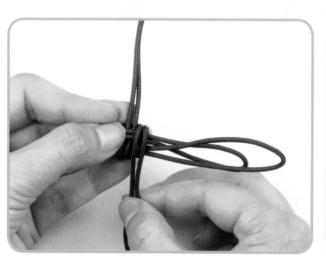

9 Continue with the center loop and fold it towards you to the right of the center.

10 Use your right fingers to loosen the base of the loops that were made with the cord ends. Take the last loop (the right loop) and thread it through these two loops.

11 Use your fingers to pull all the loops at the same time to tighten.

12 Press an awl into each corner loop to enlarge.

It was a sultry day when we came upon these Korean women weeding the grass. They dug up each weed with their tools and then placed it into a plastic bag. The long-sleeved shirts, gloves and head coverings are to protect their skin from the hot sun.

Garakji (ka-rak-jee)

This maedeup is built around your finger, so it's not surprising that it is also known as the ring knot. The finished maedeup resembles puzzle rings that were popular in the 1970's. The garakji maedeup always makes me think of Lee Soo-Kyoung (Hannah). This was her favorite maedeup, and she would spend her hour commute to and from work on the subway making garakji maedeup.

I frequently use a garakji maedeup in place of a clasp for my necklaces and bracelets. Simply slip the end garakji into the opening left between the cords before the final maedeup at the other end of the piece.

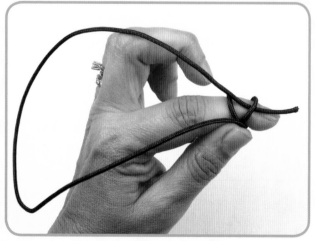

1 Use your right hand to wrap the cord around your left index finger to create an X.

2 Continue wrapping the cord around your index finger, crossing over the X.

3 Thread the cord from left to right under the upper cord, the one nearest your fingertip.

4 Turn the maedeup toward you and lift the lower cord over the upper cord.

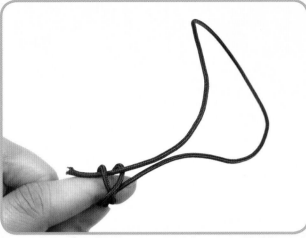

5 Use your right hand to thread the cord through the lower cord from right to left. Pull the cord snug.

6 Lift the upper cord over the lower cord.

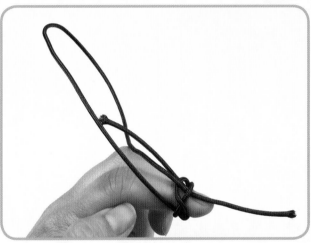

7 Thread the cord through the upper cord from left to right.

8 You will have returned to the beginning of the maedeup. Continue by threading the cord around your finger, parallel to the first cord.

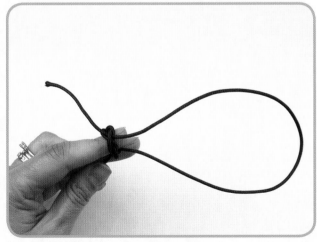

9 Continue threading the cord, following the path of the first cord. It will make parallel lines of cord.

10 Follow around until the entire maedeup has two lines of cords.

11 To tighten, pull on the end you began with to see where to start. That cord will move as you tug. Place your awl under both cords and pull to tighten. It will make two loops. Follow clockwise into the next section and place your awl under the next two cords. Pull with your awl and the loops will move from the previous section to the section you are working on. Use your left fingers and thumb to hold the maedeup as you tighten.

12 When you have gone completely around the maedeup, you will have one loop that is the end. Use your right hand to tighten that loop. It will leave a different loop to tighten.

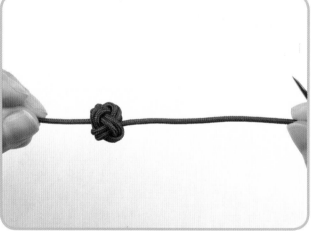

13 Use your awl to follow this cord around the maedeup, tightening as you go. I will usually tighten the garakji a second time to get it as tight as I want it to be.

14 (Optional) To make a two-cord garakji maedeup, follow the same instructions as for a one-cord maedeup through step 7. Continue with step 8, adding in the second cord and continuing with that rather than rethreading the first cord. Complete the rest of the steps using the second cord and finally tightening both cords.

Seoul is a maze of roads. If you choose to drive a car, a GPS is mandatory. My Korean girlfriends told me that Seoul's street design was intended to impede an invasion by another country. I took this picture near Ewha Women's University in Seoul.

Saengjjok (sayng-johk)

This maedeup is also known as the ginger knot due to its resemblance to the ginger root. It is also called the cloverleaf knot. It symbolizes good luck, joy and delight in life. It is also used a lot in more complicated maedeup.

1 Make a loop and anchor it with your left thumb and index finger.

2 Loop the right cord around the base of the loop and pinch it with your right thumb and index finger.

3 Release your left hand and make a loop with the left cord.

4 Thread the left loop through the right loop.

5 Use your right middle finger to anchor the loop to the top of your right index finger. Use your left hand to pull the left cord at the bottom of the loop.

6 The loop will now be under where it was originally.

7 Use your left fingers to move the loop you were holding with your right fingers, centering it over the cord and lower loop that you were holding in your right fingers.

8 Use your right fingers to take the right cord and thread it down into the top of the loop.

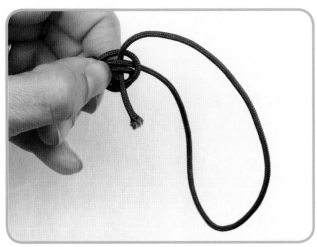

9 Continue under the two cords and back over the loop.

10 Pull the two parallel cords on each side.

11 Pull the knot tight. You will have three loops.

12 To tighten, use an awl and start at one of the side loops and follow the cording around. Continue until all three loops are tightened.

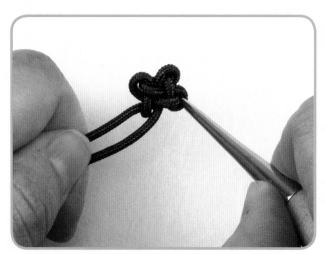

13 Press the awl into each loop to enlarge.

Saengjjok (Two-Cord Version)

The saengjjok maedeup using two cords looks a lot different from the one-cord version. Most of my jewelry designs incorporate the elegant form of saengjjok maedeup. I like to put a dorae maedeup before and after the saengjjok maedeup to help prevent it from loosening.

1 Make a loop with the purple cord and anchor it with your left thumb and index finger. Loop the pink cord around the base of the loop and pinch it with your right thumb and index finger.

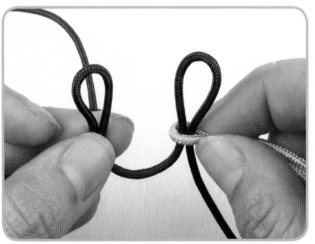

2 Release your left fingers and make another loop with the purple cord.

3 Thread this second loop through the first loop.

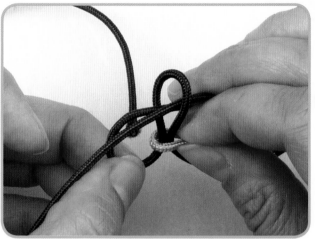

4 Use your right middle finger to anchor the loop to the top of your right index finger. Use your left hand to pull the left cord at the bottom of the loop. The loop will now be under where it was originally.

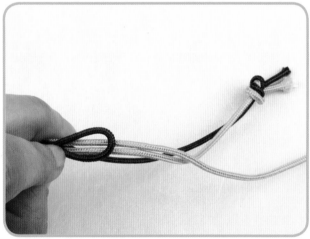

5 Use your left fingers to move the loop you were holding with your right fingers to the right, centering it over the pink cord and loop that you were holding in your right fingers.

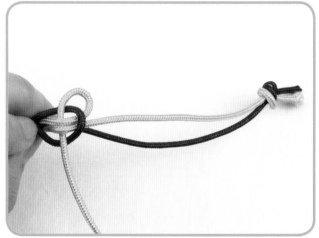

6 Use your right fingers to take the top pink cord and thread it down through the top of the loop and continue under the two pink cords and back over the loop.

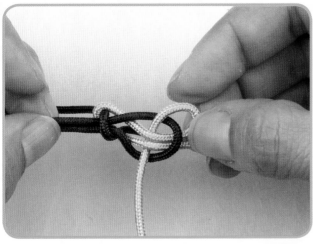

7 Pull the two parallel cords on the left (purple) and right (pink) sides of the maedeup.

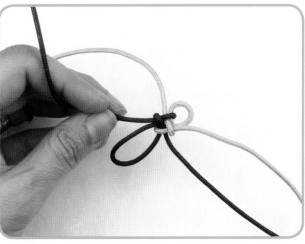

8 Pull tight. You will have three loops.

9 Now pull the pink loop and the purple loop tight.

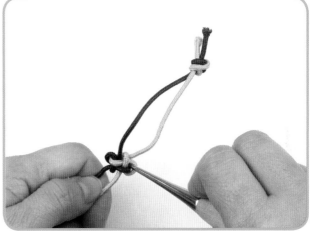

10 Tighten with an awl as you would for the saengjjok maedeup using one cord (see page 34). Press the awl into each loop to enlarge.

Sanjeongja (sahn-jeong-ja)

This is also known as the three-character knot. It is created by joining three saengjjok maedeup. I love the look of a saengjjok maedeup with a sanjeongja maedeup. It's a great combination to show off a special pendant. This maedeup can become loose, so it is best to have a maedeup such as a dorae maedeup or saengjjok maedeup on each side.

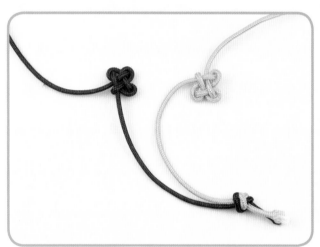

1 Using two cords, make and tighten a saengjjok maedeup on each cord (see page 32), leaving at least 2" (5cm) from the base of the cording.

2 Make a loop with the purple cord on the right side of the purple saengjjok maedeup and anchor it with your left thumb and index finger. Loop the pink cord around the base of the purple loop and pinch it with your right thumb and index finger.

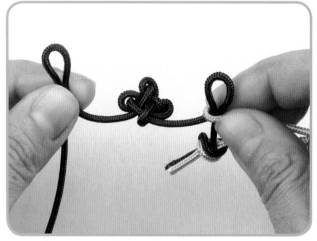

3 Make a loop with the purple cord to the left of the purple saengjjok maedeup.

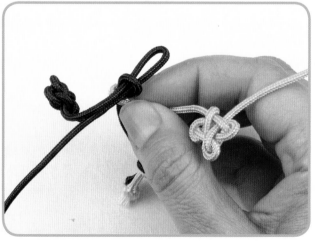

4 Thread this loop through the right purple loop.

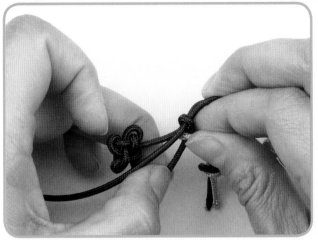

5 Use your right middle finger to anchor the loop to the top of your right index finger. Use your left hand to pull the left cord at the bottom of the loop. The loop will now be under where it was originally.

6 Use your left fingers to move the purple loop you were holding with your right fingers to the right. Center the loop over the two pink cords that you were holding in your right fingers.

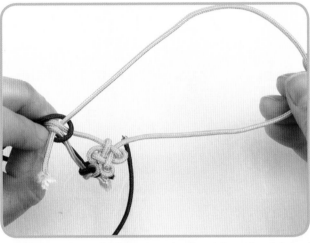

7 Use your right fingers to take the pink cord and thread it down into the top of the loop. Continue under the two pink cords and back up through the loop.

8 Pull the two parallel cords on the left (purple) and right (pink) sides. Pull them tight. You will have three loops.

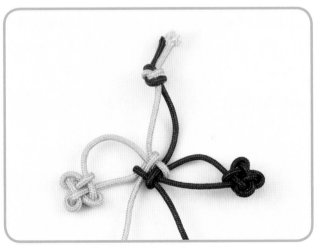

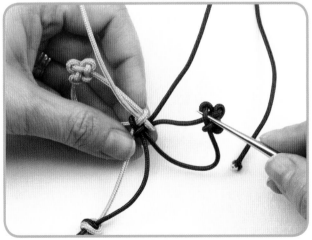

9 Use your fingers to tighten everything.

10 Turn the maedeup so the cord ends are facing away from you. Place your awl into the left cord of the purple saengjjok maedeup and loosen it so you can get a grip on the cord.

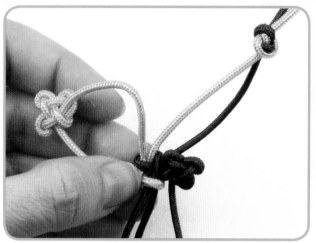

11 Use your right index finger and thumb to pull the cord while using your left index finger and thumb to secure the center knot. Pull until the purple saengjjok maedeup is tight against the center knot.

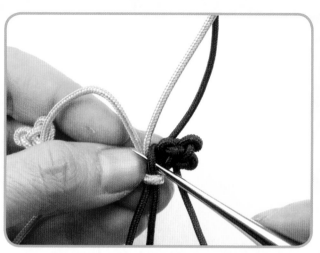

12 Tighten like a regular saengjjok maedeup. Place the awl into the right cord of the center knot.

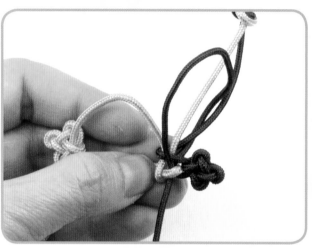

13 Tighten.

14 Pull the purple cord end to tighten.

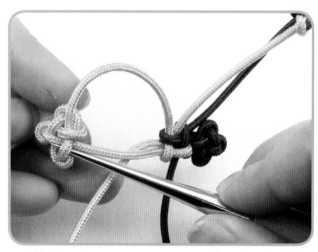

15 Place the awl into the right cord of the pink saengjjok maedeup.

16 Continue tightening the pink saengjjok maedeup as you did the purple.

Yeonbong (yun-bohng)

The yeonbong maedeup is also known as the lotus bud because it resembles that flower. The lotus flower symbolizes wealth, honor and rank. The yeonbong is also called the "button knot" and was used as a button in ancient times. A new bride's family would make yeonbong maedeup as a wedding gift for her husband. It was also thought that this was such a necessary knot in daily life that if you forgot how it was made, it was your time to die.

1 Fold the cord in half to find the center. Loop the center over your left index finger.

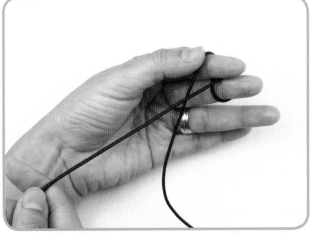

2 Use your right fingers to wrap the right cord around your left middle finger and over the left cord.

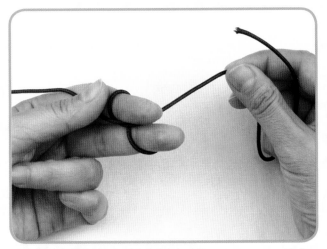

3 Bring the bottom left cord up between your two left fingers.

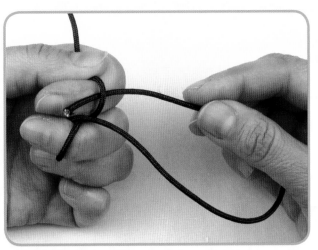

4 Take the same cord and thread it up through the back of the loop on your left index finger.

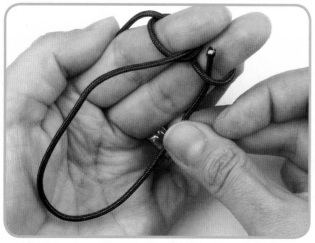

5 Take the other cord in front and thread it up through the front of the loop on your left middle finger.

6 Lift the loops off your fingers.

7 Pull the inner cords of the interlocking loops apart, which will leave one cord in the center.

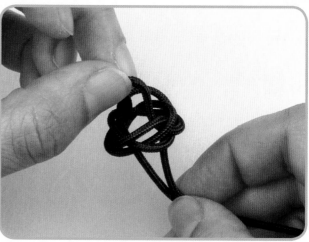

8 Use your right thumb and index finger to pull the center cord while your left thumb and index finger hold the maedeup in place.

9 Pull the center cord and each end of the cord to tighten. You will be left with a large loop in the center.

10 Loop the right cord around the back of the center loop to the front and then down through the center.

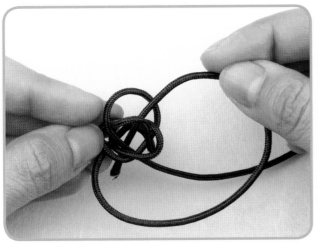

11 Loop the left cord around the front of the center loop to the back and then down through the center.

12 Take the top loop with your left fingers and the bottom cords with your right fingers. Pull to tighten.

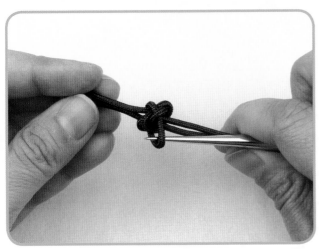

13 Push and pull on one of the two cords coming out of the bottom of the maedeup to find a starting place to tighten. Use your awl to tighten.

Yeonbong (Two-Cord Version)

I found it easier to learn the yeonbong maedeup using two different colored cords than with just one color. The two colors make following the steps easier by clearly showing you where the cording is going as you construct the maedeup. For some reason this maedeup was one of the hardest for me to learn, but I had my Korean friends, Hellena and Hannah, there to patiently help me when Su-Mi (our maedeup teacher) was busy with other students.

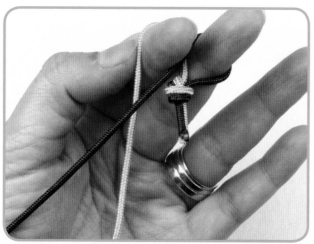

1 Place the knot between your middle finger and your index finger on your left hand, loop the pink cord up between the two fingers and around your left index finger, and loop the purple cord out around your left middle finger, through the center and to the left over the pink cord.

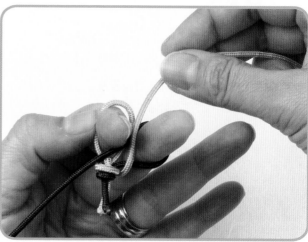

2 Loop the pink cord under the knot and between your two fingers.

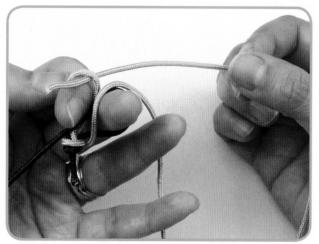

3 Thread the pink cord up through the back of the loop on your left index finger.

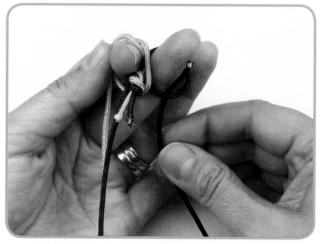

4 Take the purple cord, go under the front knot and thread it up through the front of the loop on your left middle finger.

5 Lift the loops off of your fingers. Notice that in the center there is a pink, purple and another pink cord.

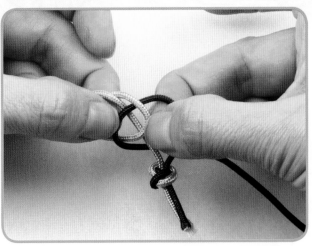

6 Pull the top two cords apart. This will leave a pink cord in the center.

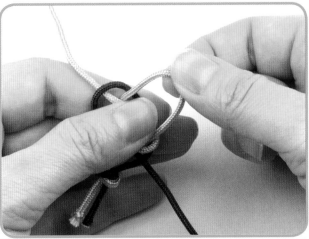

7 Pull this pink center cord up into a loop. Pinch the bottom of the pink loop using your left thumb and index finger. Pull the pink loop and each cord end to tighten the bottom loop that is under your left thumb and index finger.

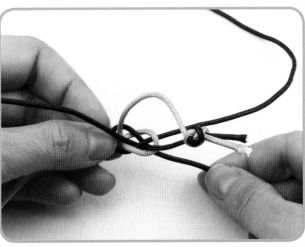

8 With your right hand, take the purple cord and wrap it around the back of the knot counterclockwise. Pull to tighten slightly. Thread through the center.

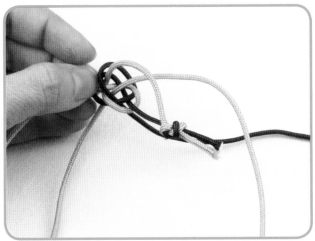

9 With your right hand, take the pink cord and wrap it around the front of the knot counterclockwise. Thread through the center. Pull to tighten slightly.

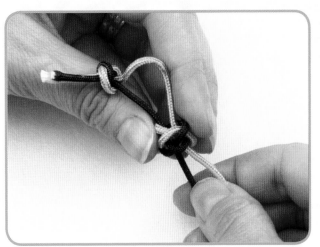

10 Pull both cord ends to tighten.

Jamjari (jahm-ja-ree)

The jamjari maedeup is also known as the dragonfly knot. It consists of a yeonbong maedeup for the head, two nalgae maedeup for the wings and a series of dorae maedeup for the body. The wings are wide and symbolize dreams that you hope will one day come true. The jamjari maedeup represents to the Korean people something precious and worthy.

1 Make a yeonbong maedeup (see page 41) and leave a loop at the top of the maedeup.

2 Turn the cord so the yeonbong maedeup is at the bottom. Cross the right cord over the left. Bring the left cord through the center, making a loop.

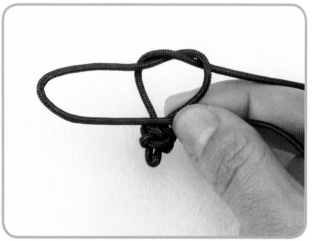

3 Take the left cord and loop it in front of the center. This is a wing.

4 Take the right cord and loop it in back of the center.

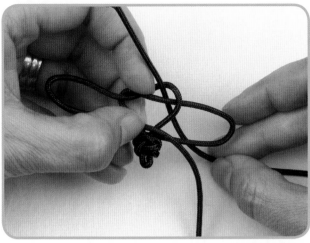

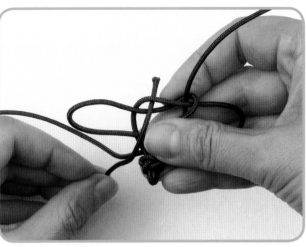

5 At the center top you will see two small center loops. Take the right cord and bring it behind the right loop and thread it up through the right center loop. Pull the cord all the way through.

6 Take the left cord and bring it in front of the left loop and thread it down through the left center loop. Pull the cord all the way through.

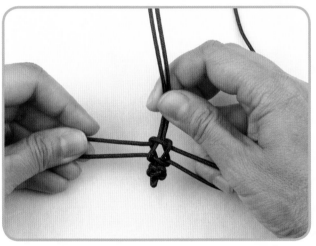

7 Pull the two loops and center two cords to tighten. Use your awl to adjust the loops to the length you want.

8 Repeat steps 2–7 to make a second set of wings slightly smaller than the first set.

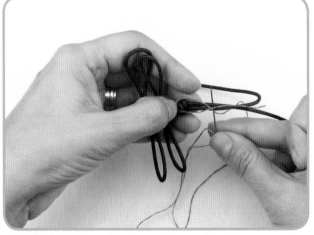

9 Make at least two dorae maedeup (see page 18). It is your decision how many dorae maedeup you wish to have.

10 Take some thread with a sewing needle and loop it over the top of the two cords.

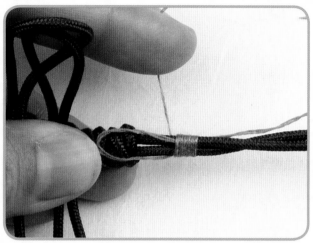

11 Wrap the thread tightly around the two cords going in the direction of the dorae maedeup. Wrap until you like the look, about ⅛" (3mm) to ¼" (6mm).

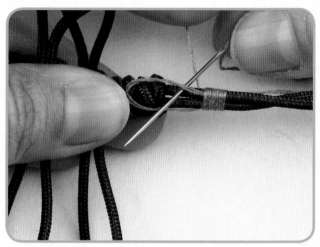

12 Thread the needle through the loop.

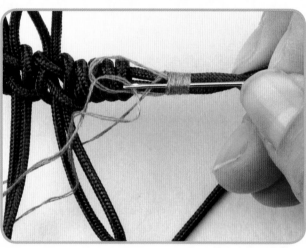

13 Thread the needle down through the wrapped thread and out the other side.

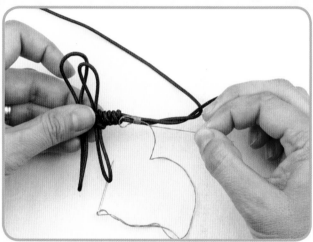

14 Pull the thread that isn't attached to the needle until the entire loop disappears. Cut off the excess thread.

TIP

A second way to finish the jamjari maedeup is to make five dorae maedeup to form the tail rather than finishing with steps 10–14.

jewelry techniques

You can complete any of the projects in this book with store-bought findings. The tough decision is choosing a component that complements and enhances the project. The options are vast, and you can find items everywhere from your local bead store or craft store to online stores. You have taken the time to create a beautiful piece of jewelry, and the right finding will make it so much more special and unique.

Opening and Closing Jump Rings

You can use flat-nose pliers or a combination of flat- and chain-nose pliers to open and close jump rings. Never open a jump ring by pulling the ends outward. This will weaken and distort the jump ring.

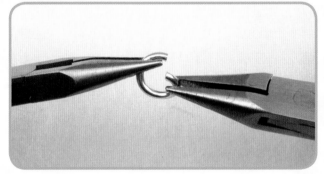

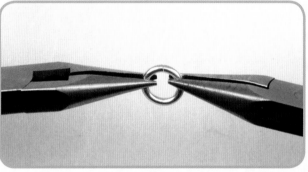

1 Use two sets of pliers to hold the jump ring on each side of the opening. Twist one side toward you as you twist the other side away from you.

2 To close, twist the sides in the opposite direction, bringing the ring ends back together.

Attaching Ear Wires

Never open the loop of an ear wire by pulling the end outward. It will weaken and distort the loop. If you find you are having difficulty opening the loop, use two sets of pliers. Place one set on the coiled section of the ear wire and the other next to the loop opening.

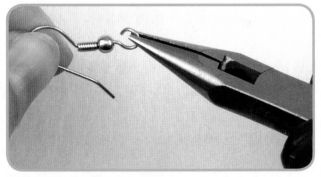

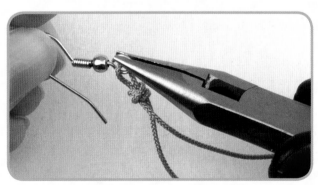

1 Use the chain-nose pliers to twist the loop either toward you or away from you to open the ear wire.

2 Place the maedeup loop in the ear wire loop. Use the chain-nose pliers to twist the loop closed. The loop will be closed completely so the maedeup cannot slip out.

Attaching a Toggle Clasp

You need three things to attach a toggle clasp: the clasp, a crimp tube and crimp pliers. Attaching a toggle clasp using a crimp tube will make your jewelry strong and durable. There are so many toggle clasps to choose from that it may be hard to decide on one. Remember, if you buy a sterling silver clasp, it will eventually tarnish and need to be cleaned. I keep my sterling silver jewelry in sealable plastic bags to slow down this process.

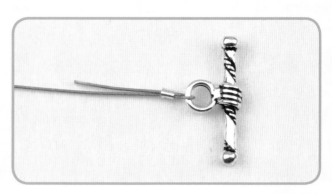

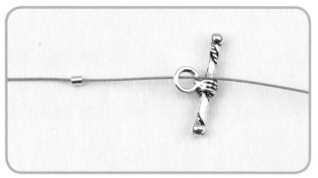

1 String a crimp tube and one half of the toggle clasp onto the beading wire.

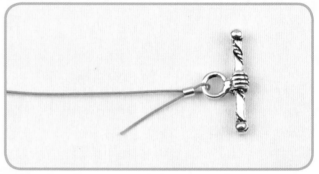

2 String the wire back through the crimp tube. Slide the tube close to the clasp.

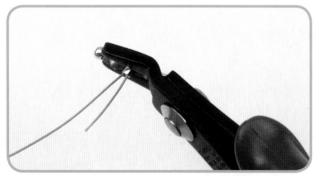

3 Place the tube into the first section (closest to the handle) of the crimp pliers and squeeze the pliers to crimp.

4 Place the tube into the second section of the crimp pliers and squeeze the pliers to complete the crimp.

Attaching a Fold-Over Crimp End

Fold-over crimp ends are a great way to finish your maedeup projects. You will need either chain-nose or flat-nose pliers to fold the crimp end. Crimp ends come in many different sizes and widths, so make sure your cording fits into the crimp end. The cords should sit side by side. I also put a drop of glue in the crimp end, but it is not mandatory.

1 Cut the cording to fit the crimp end. Dot the center of the crimp end with cyanoacrylate glue and place both cords into the crimp end. Let the glue set for a few minutes.

2 Use chain-nose pliers to fold one side of the crimp end over the cords.

3 Fold over the second side of the crimp end.

Wire Loop

A wire loop requires chain-nose (or flat-nose) pliers, round-nose pliers and flush cutters. The diameter of the loop is a matter of choice, but keep in mind that the smaller the diameter, the tougher the wire is to bend. If you have trouble, use this method to straighten your wire out again. First, use your fingers to bend it as straight as you can. Then, lay something flat over the wire, like a book or a cutting board, and roll it back and forth over the wire a few times. When you lift up the book, the wire will be straight.

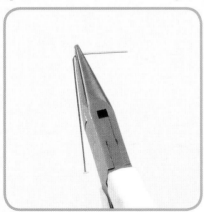 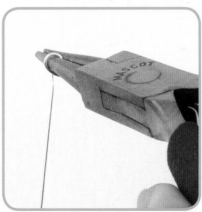 

1 Use chain-nose or flat-nose pliers to bend the wire at a 90-degree angle.

2 Use round-nose pliers to bend the wire into a loop.

3 Use flush cutters to cut off the excess wire.

PROJECTS

Maedeup is an important part of Korea's cultural history. The projects in this book take a craft that is thousands of years old and update it for the 21st century. The knots remain the same, but the purpose of the knots has changed. Knots that once adorned fans and swords are now used in elegant, contemporary jewelry.

Usually my projects begin with a focal bead or set of beads. I decide whether the piece will be a necklace, bracelet or earrings. The next step is to determine the color of cording that will best complement the bead or beads. (Sometimes this is the hardest decision for me to make. In my craft room, I have a floor-to-ceiling wardrobe rack that displays all of my maedeup cording.) I then sketch out the project with the maedeup I want to use and determine how much cording I need (see pages 16–17)—it is better to have too much than to end up short. Once I cut the cording, I'm ready to begin.

You can only master maedeup through practice. The more you repeat the steps to the maedeup, the easier it will get. I love maedeup because, if you make a mistake, you can simply untie the cord and start again. Some days in Korea I spent so much time on maedeup that my fingers and wrists ached. I took it to the extreme because I wanted to learn as much as I could while I was there. The two items needed to create maedeup (the cording and an awl) were always easy to tuck into my purse and then pull out when riding the subway in Seoul. It fascinated the Koreans, who were surprised to see a foreigner doing a native craft. It was also an icebreaker. I spoke English with a little Korean thrown in, and the older women didn't know English, but the maedeup brought us together and allowed us to communicate.

Whenever I completed a particularly difficult maedeup in class, Su-Mi, my maedeup teacher, would say to me, "Good, once more." Of course, she always had a big smile on her face. So in the words of Su-Mi, I say to you, "Good, once more."

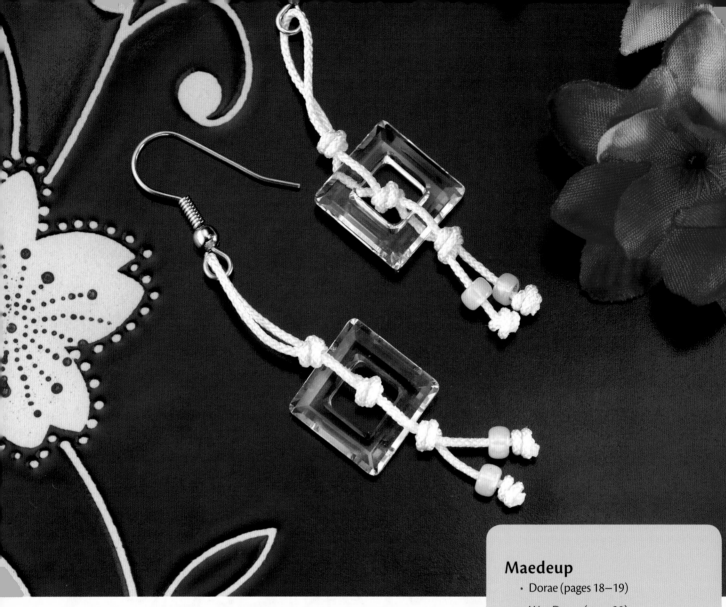

crystal square earrings

These earrings would complement any bride as she walks down the aisle. A Korean wedding is quite different from a wedding in the States. Su-Mi, my maedeup teacher, was planning her wedding during the writing of this book. For her wedding she had four dresses: two white wedding gowns (like you would wear in the U.S.), an evening gown and a *hanbok* (traditional Korean clothing). Everything is rented except for the *hanbok*, which is custom-made. One of the wedding gowns and the evening gown are worn only for wedding pictures taken before the wedding. The second wedding gown is for the wedding ceremony. The *hanbok* is worn for a traditional Korean wedding, which is a separate ceremony for family members only.

Maedeup
- Dorae (pages 18–19)
- Wae Dorae (page 20)

Materials
- 2' (61cm) 1mm white cording, cut in half
- 2 14mm crystal Swarovski squares
- 4 $^6/_0$ opal silver-lined seed beads
- 2 silver fishhook ear wires
- Ruler
- Scissors
- Glue
- Chain-nose pliers

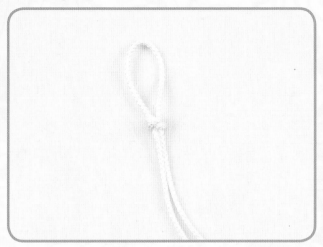

1 Fold one of the foot-long cords in half. Make a dorae maedeup ¾" (2cm) from the fold.

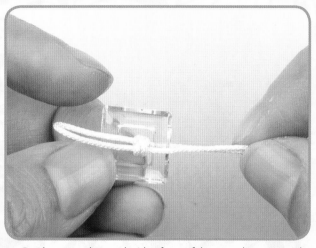

2 Place a cord on each side of one of the crystal squares with the dorae in the center of the square.

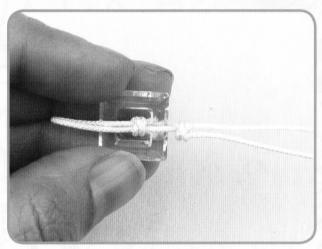

3 Make a dorae maedeup and tighten it close to the crystal square.

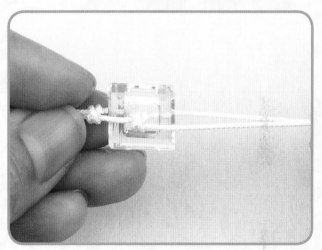

4 Flip the cording around so the dorae maedeup is in the center of the crystal square.

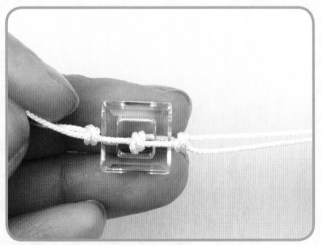

5 Make a dorae maedeup and tighten it close to the crystal square.

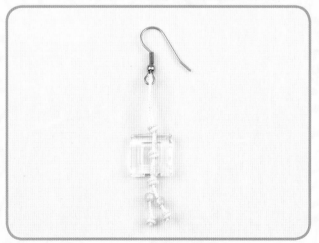

6 String a bead onto each cord end and make a wae dorae maedeup. Tighten ½" (1cm) from the previous dorae maedeup. Cut off the excess cording and glue the ends. Attach to an ear wire (see page 49). Repeat the entire process using the other cord for the second earring.

dangling saengjjok earrings

In Seoul there is a shopping center called Dongdaemun Market. Inside you will find a crafter's heaven: floors and floors of fabric, yarn, ribbons and everything else you can imagine. Thousands of individual vendors cover every floor, and they sell at wholesale prices. I had a favorite vendor who sold beautiful satin, and I paid 6000 won ($6 U.S.) a meter. The fifth floor is a sea of bead and findings vendors. I would walk by vendors displaying spools and spools of metal chains. When I found something I liked (and I always did), I would ask, "Eol-ma-ye-yo?" which means, "How much is it?" in Korean. The clerk would whip out a calculator, enter the price and turn the calculator so I could see what he had entered. *Sold*!

Maedeup
- Saengjjok (pages 32–34)

Materials
- 2' (61cm) each 1.5mm light blue, royal blue, lavender and purple cording
- 2 2¼" (6cm) 6mm × 4.5mm oval chains (10 links)
- 8 5mm 20-gauge silver jump rings
- 2 silver fishhook ear wires
- Scissors
- Awl
- Ruler
- Glue
- 2 sets of chain-nose pliers

1 Cut each cord in half. Make a saengjjok maedeup out of all eight cords. Cut ⅜" (1cm) from the end of each cord and glue the ends to prevent unraveling.

2 Use the jump rings (see page 49) to attach a saengjjok maedeup to every third link in each of the chains, alternating sides in this order: purple, light blue, lavender and royal blue. Attach each chain to an ear wire (see page 49).

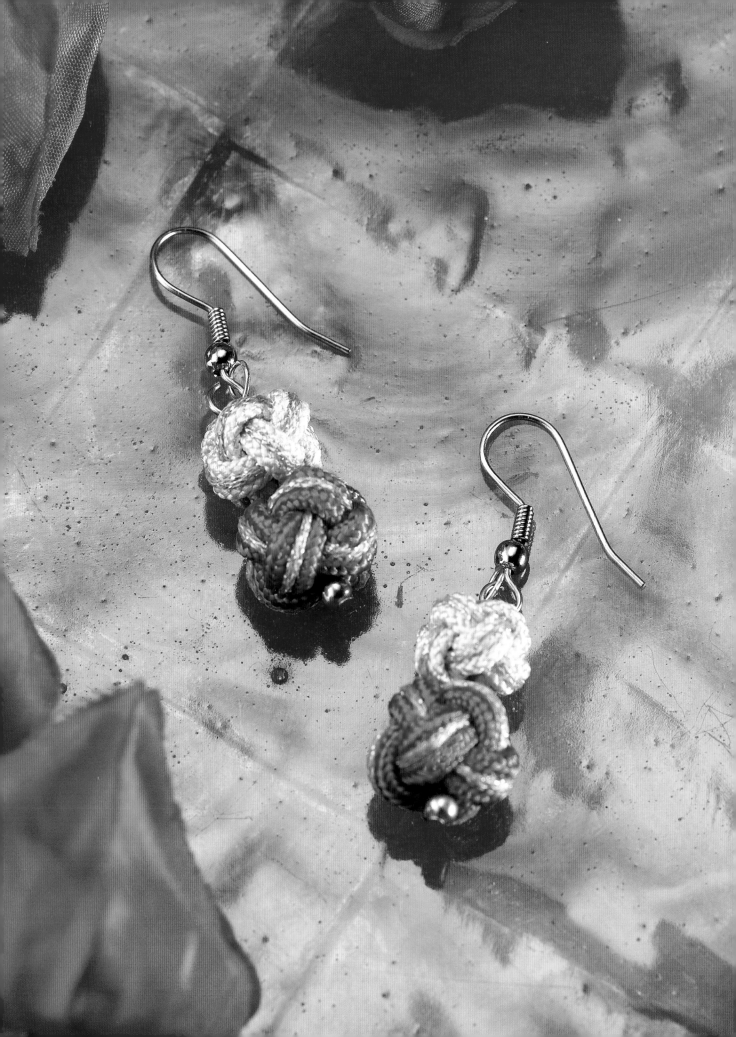

garakji with metallic thread earrings

Garakji maedeup can be easily made into earrings. I like to take cording and make up a bunch of garakji maedeup in all sizes and colors. I store them in a plastic compartment box with my other beading supplies so I always have some ready for a project.

Head pins are perfect for stringing garakji maedeup. The longer the head pin, the more garakji maedeup you can string. You can also add beads and crystals for an elegant look. I love the appearance of garakji maedeup simply strung on a head pin. Let your imagination go wild and you will be thrilled with the results.

Maedeup
- Garakji (pages 28–30)

Materials
- 2 finished turquoise metallic thread garakji maedeup (see pages 93–95)
- 2 finished light aqua metallic thread garakji maedeup
- 2 1½" (4cm) silver head pins
- 2 5mm silver beads
- 2 silver fishhook ear wires
- Chain-nose pliers
- Round-nose pliers
- Flush cutters

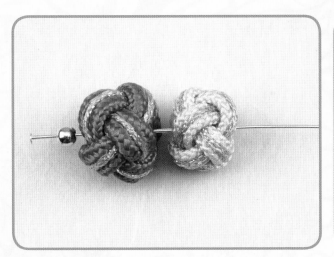

1 String a silver bead, turquoise garakji maedeup and light aqua garakji maedeup onto a head pin. Repeat for the other earring.

2 Make a loop at the end of the head pin and attach it to one of the ear wires (see page 49). Repeat for the second earring.

flattened garakji earrings

You can easily flatten garakji maedeup once you complete them. It gives the maedeup a totally different look. These earrings combine two of my favorite colors: turquoise and chartreuse. You can also make the earrings with two shades of the same color: purple and lavender, blue and light blue, or even black and gray. For yet another look, you can use the same color for both cords and a contrasting color for the center bead: purple cording with a turquoise bead or hot pink cording with an orange bead.

By using larger-diameter cording, such as 2mm, you can make an earring into a pin instead. I used one as an ornament to decorate the miniature Christmas tree we had in Korea. The pin back held it onto the tree. I decorated the entire tree in maedeup.

Maedeup
- Garakji (pages 28–30)

Materials
- 1½' (46cm) 1.2mm turquoise Chinese cording, cut in half
- 1½' (46cm) 1.2mm chartreuse Chinese cording, cut in half
- Turquoise or chartreuse thread
- 2 ⁶/₀ light green opaque luster seed beads
- 2 silver flat-pad ear studs with posts
- 2 silver/plastic earring backs
- Glue
- Ruler
- Scissors
- Sewing needle

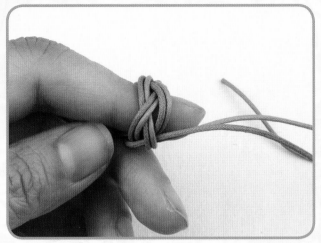

1 Using a turquoise and a chartreuse cord, make a two-cord garakji maedeup.

2 Use your fingers to flatten the garakji maedeup.

3 To tighten, start at the beginning of the garakji maedeup (where the cording entered the maedeup) and use your fingers to pull both cords in the same direction. Work around the entire maedeup. Flatten to ⅝" (2cm) diameter.

4 Take the cording from one side and thread it through the center hole. Glue the cording to the maedeup near the center hole. Let dry. Cut the cording ³⁄₁₆" (5mm) from the center.

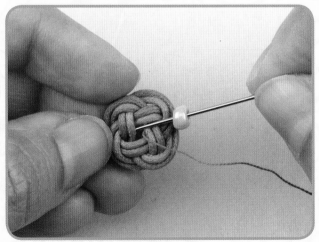

5 Thread the needle and make a knot. On the glued side of the maedeup, place the needle into the maedeup near the center and come up through the center. Thread the bead onto the needle and place the needle into the opposite side of the hole.

6 Glue an ear stud to the center of the maedeup back. Attach the earring back. Repeat the entire process for the second earring.

cloisonné earrings

The cranberry color of these earrings reminds me of fall in Korea. Blankets full of red peppers drying in the sun covered the sidewalks. Red peppers are used to make hot pepper paste (*gochujang* in Korean). *Gochujang* is a staple in the Korean diet and is used in a lot of Korean dishes. Dishes containing it can be extremely spicy depending on how much you use. In my local grocery store in Korea, choices of *gochujang* took up an entire aisle. I loved it!

Maedeup
- Dorae (pages 18–19)
- Saengjjok (pages 32–34)

Materials
- 5' (1.5 meters) 1.2mm cranberry Chinese cording, cut in half
- 2½" (1cm) cloisonné beads
- 2 silver fishhook ear wires
- Ruler
- Awl
- Scissors
- Glue
- Chain-nose pliers

1 Fold one of the cords in half and make a dorae maedeup ¼" (6mm) from the fold. Make a saengjjok maedeup.

2 Thread both ends of the cord through the cloisonné bead and make a dorae maedeup. Cut off the excess cording and glue the end. Attach an ear wire (see page 49). Repeat the entire process for the other earring.

yeonbong earrings

You can really have fun with maedeup when you combine it with lampwork beads. Lampwork beads come in all shapes and sizes, which is just the incentive to let your imagination run wild. Lampworkers make up a wonderful community, and many have become friends of mine. I have made lampwork beads and can attest to how difficult it is just to make a round bead.

These earrings are fun to make and a good way to practice the yeonbong maedeup while making a classy project. The lampwork beads take center stage and stand out with the help of maedeup. For a different look, you can cut the cording off at the end of the second yeonbong maedeup, leaving out the Czech glass beads.

Maedeup
- Yeonbong (pages 41–43)
- Wae Dorae (page 20)

Materials
- 2 yrds. (1.8 meters) 2mm black Korean cording, cut in half
- 2 22mm × 10mm (minimum 3.5mm hole) lampwork beads (Canterbury Keepsakes, see page 126)
- 4 6mm topaz matte Czech glass beads
- 2 6mm gold-plated jump rings
- 2 gold-plated kidney ear wires
- Ruler
- Awl
- Scissors
- Glue
- 2 sets of chain-nose pliers

1 Fold a cord in half and make a one-cord yeonbong. When tightening, leave a ¼" (6mm) loop at the top. Thread a lampwork bead.

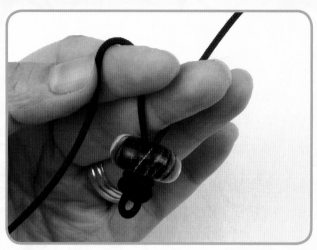

2 Place the bead between the index and middle fingers of your left hand. Thread the right cord between your middle and ring fingers. Loop the left cord up between your index and middle fingers and around the index finger.

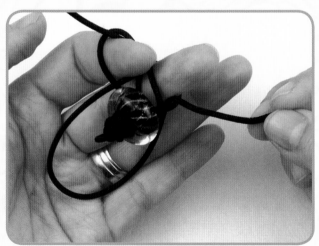

3 Wrap the right cord around your middle finger and down between it and your index finger, crossing over the other cord.

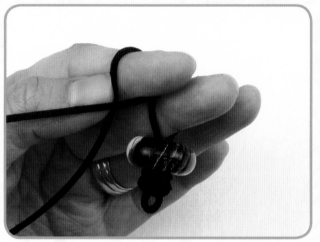

4 Loop the other cord around the bead and up between your index and middle fingers.

5 Thread the same cord up through the loop on the back of your index finger. Loop the other cord behind the bead and up through the front loop on your middle finger. Finish with steps 8–10 of *Yeonbong Maedeup (Two-Cord Version)* on page 45.

6 Thread a glass bead onto each cord end. Make a wae dorae maedeup and tighten ½" (1cm) from the yeonbong. Cut off the excess cording and glue the ends. Attach a jump ring and an ear wire (see page 49). Repeat the entire process for the other earring.

chinese coin earrings

China seems to be the originator of coins with square holes in the center. None of their current coins contain a hole, but two coins used today in Japan do. Korea never put a hole in its currency. If you ever visit a Chinatown, lots of vendors sell replicas of such coins. You can also find them on the Internet.

The hemp cording in this project has a sleek coating, so the maedeup may loosen as you make the earrings. All you need to do is go back and retighten the maedeup. You may also need to do this when working with satin cording.

Maedeup

- Dorae (pages 18–19)
- Saengjjok (pages 32–34)
- Sanjeongja (pages 38–40)

Materials

- 3' (92cm) 1mm green hemp cording, cut in half
- 2 19.5mm × 14.5m × 2mm sterling silver Chinese coin charms (Nina Designs, see page 126)
- 2 silver fishhook ear wires
- Ruler
- Awl
- Scissors
- Glue

1 Thread an ear wire onto one cord and fold the cording in half. Keep the ear wire near the fold and make a dorae maedeup ⅜" (1cm) from the fold. Continue with a saengjjok maedeup.

2 Make a sanjeongja maedeup. Thread a coin onto both cords. Make a dorae maedeup. Loop around the two cords coming down from the saengjjok maedeup instead of the usual one cord. Finish as for a regular dorae maedeup and tighten, leaving a ³⁄₁₆" (5mm) loop.

3 Cut off the excess cording and glue the end. Repeat the entire process for the other earring.

dongsimgyeol earrings

South Koreans are big on giving gifts for any occasion. Whenever a couple invited us to dinner, they brought a gift, such as a plant or a bottle of wine. If you visit another country for vacation or work, it is customary to bring back a gift.

Whenever we visited friends and family in the United States, I brought back gifts for all my Korean friends. We bought American chocolate for my husband's co-workers, which was always appreciated. I also made a maedeup necklace or bracelet for each guest who visited us from the U.S. These earrings make a perfect gift for starting the gift tradition in your life.

Maedeup
- Dongsimgyeol (pages 24–27)
- Wae Dorae (page 20)

Materials
- 1½' (46cm) 1.5mm fuchsia Korean cording, cut in half
- 14 ⁶/₀ ruby frosted aurora borealis transparent seed beads
- 2 silver flat-pad ear studs with posts
- 2 silver/plastic earring backs
- Awl
- Ruler
- Scissors
- Glue

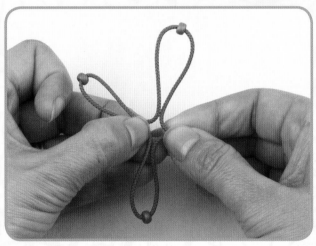

1 String 3 seed beads onto one of the cords. Fold the cording in half to find the center. Make 3 1½" (4cm) loops for the dongsimgyeol maedeup with 1 bead in each loop.

2 Complete the dongsimgyeol maedeup. String 2 beads on each cord end. Make a wae dorae maedeup on each cord and tighten ½" (1cm) from the dongsimgyeol maedeup. Cut off the excess cording and glue the tips.

3 Glue an ear stud to the back of the earring (where the cords are coming out of the maedeup). Repeat the entire process for the second earring.

dragonfly earrings

During the hot summers in South Korea, I would look out our living room window to be greeted by dozens of dragonflies. What was so amazing to me was that our apartment was on the tenth floor!

In Korea, dragonflies (*jamjari* in Korean) symbolize courage and strength. I have found a new appreciation for dragonflies. I had always been terrified of them in the past, but living in Korea taught me to appreciate the dragonfly for what it symbolizes.

You can make these earrings using other media for the square. If you have some polymer clay or wooden squares in your craft stash, you can always substitute one of those.

Maedeup

- Jamjari (pages 46–48)

Materials

- 3' (1 meter) 1mm lavender Korean cording, cut in half
- 2⅞" (2cm) violet metal squares with holes
- Lavender thread
- 2 5mm 20-gauge silver jump rings
- 2 silver fishhook ear wires
- Ruler
- Awl
- Sewing needle
- Scissors
- Glue
- Chain-nose pliers

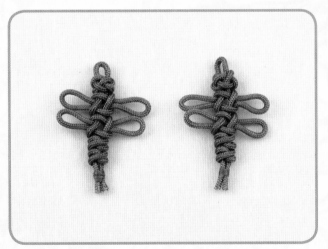

1 Make 2 jamjari maedeup with loops measuring ¼" (6mm) long. Finish with 2 dorae maedeup. Use thread to finish.

2 Glue one jamjari maedeup to the center of each metal square. Let dry. Attach the jump rings and ear wires (see page 49).

dorae and coiled wire watch

Prior to moving to South Korea, I never left home without wearing a watch. Once there, I noticed while riding the buses and subway that Koreans used their cell phones (called hand phones in Korea) to check the time. Their cell phones were always in their hands, and they did a lot of texting. I was amazed at how fast their fingers flew over the phone keyboards.

This watch shows how well maedeup complements other media such as wire. Keep in mind that you can adjust the number of coils and maedeup to fit your own wrist. However, if you add or subtract sections, you will need to be consistent with each of the four lengths of the watch band.

Maedeup
- Dorae (pages 18–19)

Materials
- 7' (2.1 meters) 24-gauge black craft wire
- 16' (5 meters) 1.5mm gray Korean cording, cut in 4 pieces
- 1" (25mm) square watch face
- 2 large (3.5mm × 11mm × 5mm) fold-over crimp ends
- 2 5mm 20-gauge silver jump rings
- Sterling silver toggle clasp
- 2 sets of chain-nose pliers
- Flush cutter
- Ruler
- Paintbrush
- Scissors
- Glue

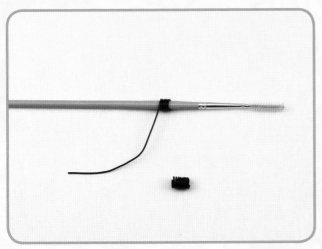

1 Cut the black wire into 14 6" (15cm) pieces. Wrap each wire around a paintbrush to make a coil. Set aside.

2 Thread the cord through the watch face and move the watch face to the center of the cord. Make 2 dorae maedeup.

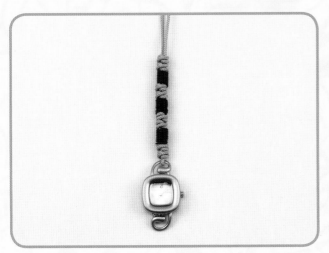

3 Thread a coil and make 2 dorae maedeup. Repeat twice more.

4 Add a second cord to the same side of the watch. Repeat step 3 three times. Add a final coil. Repeat steps 2–4 for the other side of the watch face.

5 Attach the crimp ends, jump rings and toggle clasp (see pages 49–51). Trim the cord ends.

dorae bracelet

This dorae bracelet complements the dorae necklace on page 86. I have always had an obsession for bracelets. A girl just can't have too many. You can also wear this bracelet with other silver bracelets to really make the maedeup stand out. I love to wear more than one bracelet at a time.

You can easily adjust the bracelet to fit any wrist. Add or subtract dorae maedeup to make it larger or smaller. Remember the garakji maedeup in your calculations when adjusting the length of the bracelet. The yeonbong maedeup is slightly smaller but would look just as great in place of the garakji maedeup.

Maedeup

- Dorae (pages 18–19)
- Garakji (pages 28–30)

Materials

- 19½' (6 meters) 1.5mm black Chinese cording, cut in half
- 3 10.2mm (minimum 3mm hole) sterling silver beads (Nina Designs, see page 126)
- Ruler
- Awl
- Scissors
- Glue

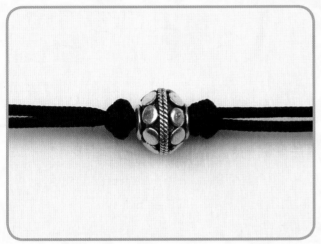

1 Thread a bead onto both cords. Fold the cording in half to find the center and move the bead to the center. Make a dorae maedeup on each side of the bead to anchor the bead in the center.

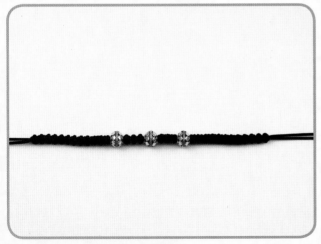

2 Make 2 more dorae maedeup on each side. Thread a bead and make 12 dorae maedeup on each side.

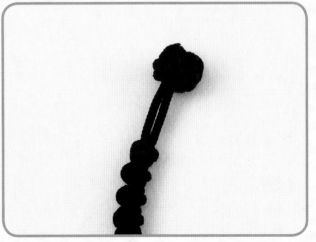

3 Make a garakji maedeup 1" (3cm) from the last dorae maedeup. When tightening the garakji maedeup, leave a ¾" (2cm) space between the last dorae maedeup and the garakji maedeup. Repeat for the opposite side. Cut off the excess cording and glue the ends.

hapjong jade bracelet

Whenever I see jade I think of Asia. Korea has a rich history with jade. It is regarded as a symbol of the five principles that all men should live by: benevolence, righteousness, wisdom, bravery and acuteness. I was fortunate and honored to meet a Korean jade craftsman who had spent his entire life carving jade. His work was incredible.

This bracelet is a quick and easy project that can be completed in an afternoon, and you can wear it out the same evening. If you want to jazz it up a bit, attach a few charms to one end of the bracelet.

Maedeup
- Hapjong (page 21)

Materials
- 3½′ (1 meter) 1.5mm dark forest green cording
- 3½′ (1 meter) 1.5mm light forest green cording
- 5 ¾″ (2cm) (minimum 3mm hole) jade barrel beads
- 2 large (approximately 3.5mm × 11mm × 5mm) fold-over crimp ends
- 2 5mm 20-gauge silver jump rings
- Sterling silver toggle clasp
- 2 sets of chain-nose pliers
- Scissors
- Glue

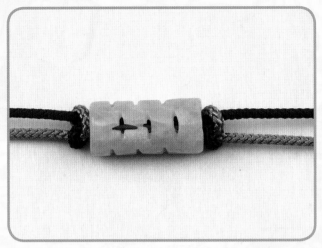

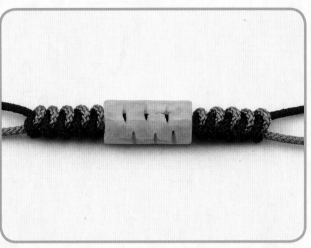

1 Thread a jade bead onto both cords, fold the cording in half to find the center and move the bead to the center. Make a hapjong maedeup on each side of the bead to anchor the bead in the center of the bracelet.

2 Make 4 additional hapjong maedeup on each side of the jade bead.

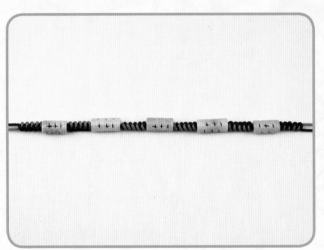

3 Thread a jade bead and make 5 hapjong maedeup twice. Repeat for the opposite side.

4 Attach the crimp ends, jump rings and toggle clasp to both ends of the bracelet (see pages 49–51). Trim the cord ends.

nalgae suede bracelet

This bracelet is a blast from the past. The '70s were full of suede items: jewelry, skirts, belts and purses, just to name a few. As a teenager I wore a suede headband and loved my suede purse with fringe on the bottom. On weekends my friend and I would drive up to Alpine Valley in East Troy, Wisconsin and sit under the stars to watch some of the biggest bands of the day: Styx, REO Speedwagon and Cheap Trick. Those were the days.

Maedeup

- Nalgae (pages 22–23)

Materials

- 8' (2.4 meters) ⅛" (3.2mm) dark brown suede lace, cut in half
- 14 frosted yellow pony beads
- 2 (8mm × 9mm) fold-over crimp ends
- 2 5mm 20-gauge silver jump rings
- Sterling silver toggle clasp
- 2 sets of chain-nose pliers
- Glue
- Scissors

1 Crimp together one end of each lace in a fold-over crimp end (see page 51). Make a nalgae maedeup. Thread a pony bead onto each lace and make another nalgae maedeup 7 times.

2 Attach a fold-over crimp end to the end of both laces. Attach the jump rings and toggle clasp to both ends (see *Opening and Closing Jump Rings*, page 49, and *Attaching a Toggle Clasp*, page 50).

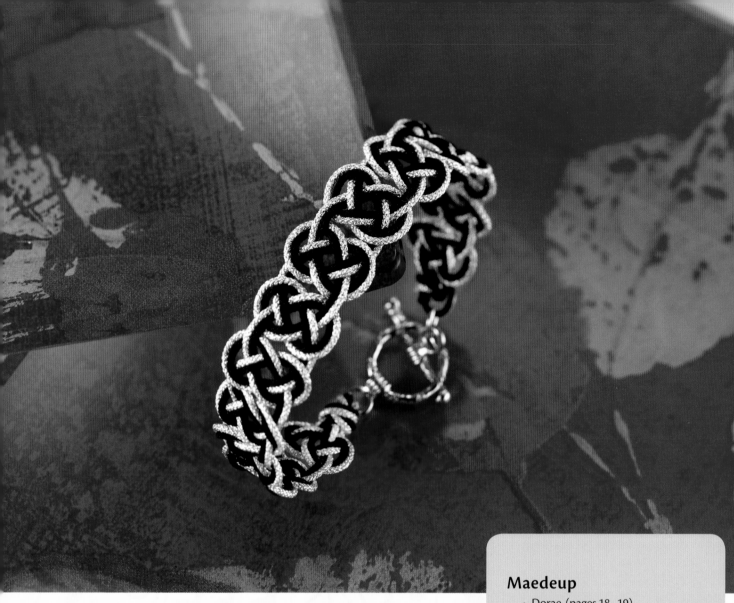

elegant nalgae bracelet

Making this bracelet requires much concentration. The center lines of the bracelet form a zigzag pattern, and you have to pay attention to the alternations. I like to watch television as I work on my maedeup, which can distract me. I know the simple solution would be to just shut off the television, right?

Wrong! While living in South Korea, I became hooked on Korean dramas. They are very different from soap operas in the United States. Korean dramas typically have sixteen episodes, unlike American soaps that can last for decades. They involve a love triangle, and someone always gets sick or hurt. Two of my all-time favorites are *My Lovely Sam-Soon* and *Full House*. I learned a lot about Korean culture watching these dramas—and my Korean improved, which was an added bonus.

Maedeup
- Dorae (pages 18–19)
- Nalgae (pages 22–23)

Materials
- 9' (2.7 meters) 1mm black Korean cording
- 9' (2.7 meters) 1mm silver Korean cording
- 2 5mm 20-gauge silver jump rings
- Sterling silver toggle clasp
- 2 pairs of chain-nose pliers
- Scissors
- Glue

1 Fold the two pieces of cording in half and make a simple knot, joining the cords together. Loop two cords over the other cords and make a dorae maedeup.

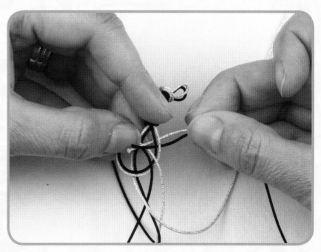

2 With the silver cord on the outside, make a nalgae maedeup.

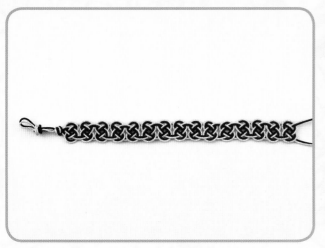

3 Make a total of 15 nalgae maedeup.

4 Make a dorae maedeup. Tighten close to the last nalgae maedeup.

5 Attach a jump ring (see page 49) and half of the toggle clasp (see page 50) to two of the cords in the dorae maedeup. Repeat for the other end of the bracelet. Retighten the dorae maedeup on both ends. Cut off the excess cording and glue the ends.

Maedeup
- Garakji (pages 28–30)

Materials
- 13½' (4.1 meters) 2mm lavender Korean cording
- 3 full loops of memory wire
- 7 grams $^{11}/_0$ ceylon-lined light lilac Delica beads
- 30 8mm Swarovski bicone crystals
- Lavender thread
- Sewing needle
- Scissors
- Glue
- Awl
- Round-nose pliers
- Flush cutter

beaded garakji memory bracelet

I was looking at a garakji maedeup I had just made and wondering how I could jazz it up a little. I was sitting in my craft room at the time with my eyes wandering around the room when they came to rest on my bead boxes. I opened up my Delica bead box and knew I had found the solution. The Delica beads are perfect for this project because they are identical and line up perfectly in each section of the garakji maedeup. The beads help to show off the multidimensional aspect of the garakji maedeup. Memory wire makes the bracelet a perfect fit for any wrist, and I love to use Swarovski crystals to add a little glitz and glamour.

1 Make 14 garakji maedeup.

2 Cut the garakji maedeup apart. Thread the needle and knot the thread. Find the beginning of the garakji maedeup by pushing and pulling on one of the two cords. Thread the needle through the end and up through the beginning of the first section.

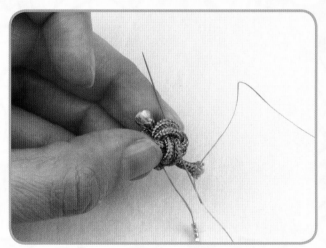

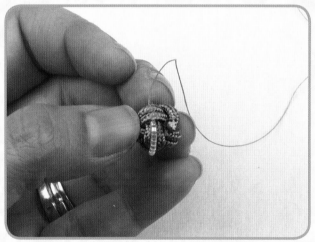

3 String enough beads to cover that section of the garakji maedeup. Thread the needle into the next section.

4 Pull the thread tight so the beads are centered in the section. Repeat steps 3–4 until all sections are beaded.

5 Knot and cut the excess thread. Cut off the excess cording and glue the ends. When dry, use your awl to enlarge the hole through each end. Use the round-nose pliers to turn one end of the memory wire into a loop. String 2 crystals and a garakji maedeup. Repeat 13 more times. String 2 crystals. Finish with another loop. Cut off any excess wire.

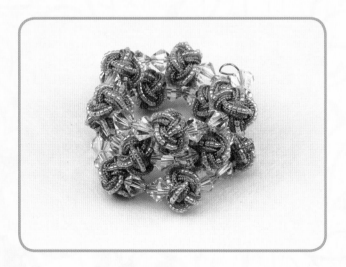

yeonbong bracelet

The blue in this bracelet reminds me of the beautiful blue skies of Korea. I never knew how mountainous Korea was until I moved there. We lived in a city just south of Seoul called Suwon. There were mountains within walking distance of our apartment. We also had a clear view of a mountain from our living room. The mountains were so beautiful up against a clear blue sky.

Hiking in the mountains is a popular Korean pastime. Koreans dress in hiking outfits complete with backpacks and hiking sticks. I even saw hikers on the streets and subways of downtown Seoul on their way to or from a mountain. They would hike in all sorts of weather, from humid 90-degree days to freezing winter days.

Maedeup
- Yeonbong (pages 41–43)

Materials
- 7' (2.1 meters) 2mm light blue Korean cording
- 36 9mm crystal aurora borealis glass ring beads
- Awl
- Ruler
- Scissors
- Glue

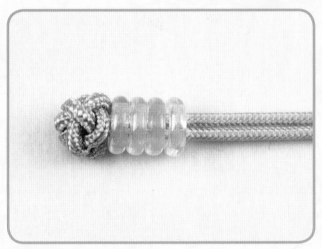

1 Fold the cording in half and make a yeonbong maedeup. Thread 4 ring beads.

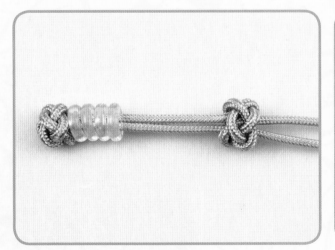

2 Make another yeonbong maedeup. Tighten against the ring beads. Thread 4 more ring beads.

3 Continue the pattern for a total of 10 yeonbong maedeup and 9 segments of ring beads ending with a yeonbong maedeup. Tighten the final yeonbong maedeup, leaving a ½" (1cm) space for the loop. Cut off the excess cording and glue the ends.

dorae necklace

The color black never goes out of style, especially when you pair it with sterling silver. The consecutive dorae maedeup in this necklace make for a chic and classic look. I was working on this necklace on a return flight from Minnesota to South Korea. The flight attendants were full of amazement and questions as they observed me through the 14-hour flight. Maedeup is great for a long airplane ride, but remember to put your awl in your checked luggage. It won't be allowed on a plane. I brought some bobby pins for the flight and they worked well in place of my awl.

Maedeup
- Dorae (pages 18–19)
- Garakji (pages 28–30)

Materials
- 24' (7.2 meters) 1.5mm black Chinese cording, cut in half
- 16.5mm (minimum 3mm hole) sterling silver focal bead (Nina Designs, see page 126)
- 6 10.2mm (minimum 3mm hole) sterling silver beads (Nina Designs, see page 126)
- Ruler
- Awl
- Scissors
- Glue

1 Thread the focal bead onto both cords. Fold the cording in half to find the center and move the bead to the center. Make a dorae maedeup on each side of the bead to anchor the bead in the center of the necklace.

2 Make 10 additional dorae maedeup on each side of the focal bead. Make each maedeup right next to the previous maedeup.

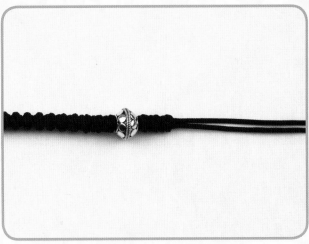

3 Thread a 10.2mm bead and make 12 dorae maedeup. String another 10.2mm bead and make 12 dorae maedeup. Repeat for the opposite side.

4 Thread a 10.2mm bead and make 3 dorae maedeup. Repeat for the opposite side.

5 Make a garakji maedeup 1" (3cm) from the last dorae maedeup. When tightening the garakji maedeup, leave a ¾" (2cm) space between the last dorae maedeup and the garakji maedeup. Repeat for the opposite side. Cut off the excess cording and glue the ends.

dorae lampwork bead necklace

If I were to describe little girls in Korea, I would use only one word: *pink*. Korean moms dress their little girls in a lot of pink. Whenever I asked a Korean girl what her favorite color was, the answer was "pink." But pink is not a "girl color." I saw many little boys wearing pink sweaters and jackets—even pink backpacks. (Of course, these could have been hand-me-downs from older sisters.) Korean men also like to wear pink. This necklace is for all the little girls of Korea.

Maedeup

- Dorae (pages 18–19)

Materials

- 12' (3.6 meters) 1.5mm dusty rose cording, cut in half
- 1" (2.5cm) (minimum 4mm hole) donut lampwork bead (Kim Miles, see page 126)
- 2 large (approximately 3.5mm × 11mm × 5mm) fold-over crimp ends
- 2 5mm 20-gauge silver jump rings
- Sterling silver toggle clasp
- 2 sets of chain-nose pliers
- Ruler
- Scissors
- Glue

1 Thread one cord through the center of the donut bead, move the bead to the center of the cord and make a dorae maedeup. Tighten close to the bead.

2 Make an additional 5 dorae maedeup.

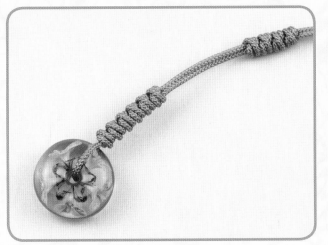

3 Measure 1¼" (3cm) and make 4 more dorae maedeup. Repeat 3 times. Measure 1¼" (3cm) from the last dorae maedeup and make 1 dorae maedeup. Repeat steps 1–3 for the second cord.

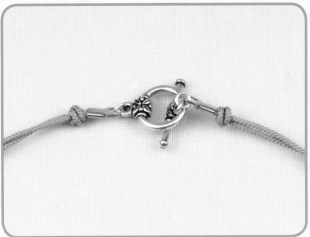

4 Attach the crimp ends, jump rings and toggle clasp to both ends of the necklace (see pages 49–51).

My cousin's twin girls wearing their traditional Korean hanbok (in pink, of course!).

hapjong sunflower necklace

Orange and yellow always remind me of a warm, sunny day. Growing up, I spent hot summer days running through a sprinkler and eating popsicles. Korean summers were brutal for this Minnesota girl. We had only one car, so I would walk to the grocery store, which was three-quarters of a mile away. I would be dripping sweat when I finally got to the air-conditioned entrance. (What puzzles me to this day is that I never saw a Korean sweating like I did.) I would also sometimes forget that I didn't have a car and would buy too many groceries. Many times I lugged full, heavy bags home, telling myself that it would never happen again, but it would.

Maedeup
- Hapjong (page 21)
- Garakji (pages 28–30)

Materials
- 10' (3 meters) 1.5mm yellow cording
- 10' (3 meters) 1.5mm orange cording
- 1¼" × 1⅜" (3.2cm × 3.5cm) polymer clay sunflower pendant (Block Party Press, see page 126)
- Awl
- Ruler
- Scissors
- Glue

1 Thread the pendant onto both cords. Fold the cords in half to find the center and move the pendant to the center. Make a hapjong maedeup on each side of the pendant to anchor the pendant in the center.

2 Make 5 additional hapjong maedeup on each side of the pendant.

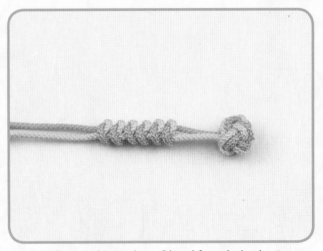

3 Use a ruler to measure 1" (3cm) from the last hapjong maedeup and make 6 hapjong maedeup. Repeat 8 additional times on both sides of the pendant.

4 Make a garakji maedeup 1" (3cm) from the last hapjong maedeup. When tightening the garakji maedeup, leave a ½" (1cm) space between the last hapjong maedeup and the garakji maedeup.

5 Repeat step 4 for the opposite side. Cut off the excess cording and glue the ends.

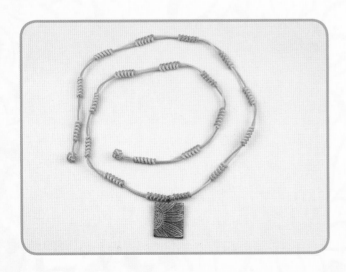

garakji with metallic thread necklace

In this project you make the garakji maedeup one after another. It's easiest to tighten each garakji maedeup as you make it, leaving about 1" (3cm) of loose cording before the next knot. Once you've finished making all of them, you highlight them with metallic thread. A loop turner makes manipulating the metallic thread easier, but if you can't locate one, you can always substitute a needle with a blunt end. Finally, you cut the garakji maedeup apart before putting them on the rubber necklace. The knots would also look fantastic strung on a silver chain.

Maedeup
- Garakji (pages 28–30)

Materials
- 10' (3 meters) 2mm turquoise cording
- 9' (2.7 meters) 1.5mm light aqua cording
- 12' (3.6 meters) Kreinik 094 star blue medium no. 16 metallic braid, cut in half (Kreinik, see page 126)
- 18" (46cm) 2mm turquoise rubber necklace
- Awl
- Loop turner
- Scissors
- Toothpick
- Glue

1 Make the following garakji maedeup: 7 in turquoise and 10 in light aqua.

2 Find the beginning of one of the garakji maedeup by pulling and pushing on one end of it. Following from the end of the cord, insert the loop turner through the center of the maedeup and into this section. Place one end of the metallic braid into the loop turner.

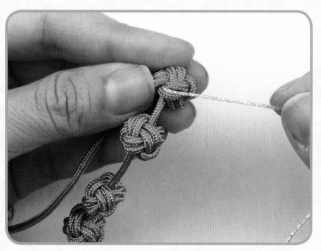

3 Pull the braid through, leaving about a 1" (3cm) tail.

4 Insert the loop turner into the next section with the point coming out of the previous section.

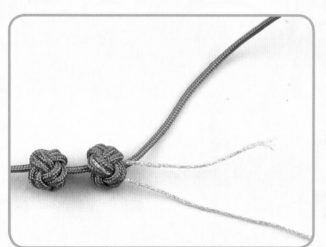

5 Place the end of the braid into the loop turner and bring it under into the next section and pull tight. Continue until the entire garakji maedeup is complete. Continue on to the next garakji maedeup. There is no need to cut the metallic braid between garakji maedeup. Do the same with the light aqua cording and second metallic braid.

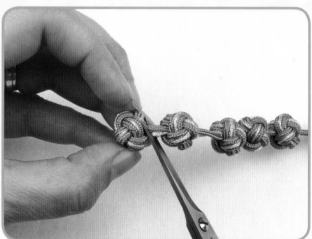

6 Cut the garakji maedeup apart.

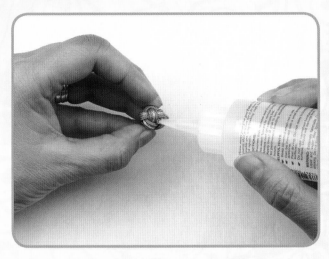

7 Glue both ends of each garakji maedeup.

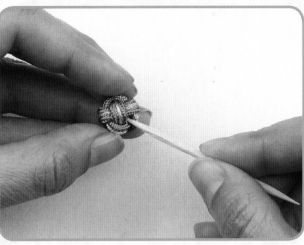

8 Use a toothpick to press the ends into the inside. Let dry for a few minutes.

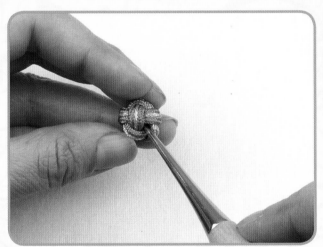

9 Use an awl to make the openings at both ends larger.

10 Thread the garakji maedeup onto the necklace: 5 light aqua, 7 turquoise and 5 light aqua.

dongsimgyeol ribbon necklace

You don't need an awl for the dongsimgyeol maedeup, so tightening is a breeze. When constructing the maedeup, you can experiment with the loop lengths. You can also leave the ends uncut for a different look. Try adding a bead to the center of the maedeup to give it a focal point. Beads are a great way to embellish maedeup. You can also use a piece of leather or strand of beads in place of the ribbon. This is an easy project, and it can be completed in a few short hours.

Maedeup
- Dongsimgyeol (pages 24–27)

Materials
- 3' (1 meter) 2mm light olive green Korean cording
- 16" (41cm) ½" (1.3cm) wide autumn leaf silk ribbon, cut in half (KAS, see page 126)
- 2 15mm silver pinch clasps
- 2 5mm silver jump rings
- Sterling silver toggle clasp
- Scissors
- Glue
- Loop turner
- Paper towel or piece of scrap fabric
- Chain-nose pliers

1 Make a dongsimgyeol maedeup with 2" (5cm) loops. The finished loops should be about ⅝" (1.6cm) long. Cut off the excess cording and glue the tips.

2 On the wrong side of the dongsimgyeol maedeup (the side with the cord ends), place the loop turner through the upper half, then place the ribbon into the holder and pull it through until the knot is centered on the ribbon. Repeat with the second ribbon.

3 Measure 7" (18cm) from the center to the end of each ribbon and cut off the excess. Place both ribbon ends on one side into a pinch clasp, cover the clasp with fabric or a paper towel (to protect the surface from marks) and use the pliers to close. Repeat with the other side. Attach the jump rings and toggle clasp to both ends (see pages 49–50).

dongsimgyeol beaded necklace

There is a wholesale jewelry market located in Namdaemun Market in Seoul called Mesa Shopping Center. In the basement you will find booth upon booth of gemstones and sterling silver findings at great prices. I bought the zoisite nuggets and sterling silver findings for this necklace at Mesa. If you ever visit, bring lots of *won* (Korean currency) because they do not take credit cards.

According to tradition, zoisite nuggets inspire love and provide a protective shield that brings economic stability. They also have the power to heal the circulatory system and alleviate pain.

You can substitute a jamjari maedeup for the dongsimgyeol maedeup and it will look just as gorgeous. This necklace would also look great as a choker.

Maedeup
- Dongsimgyeol (pages 24–27)

Materials
- 3' (1 meter) 2mm medium forest green Korean cording
- 4' (1.2 meters) .015" (0.4mm) diameter 49-strand nylon-coated flexible beading wire
- 2 3mm sterling silver balls
- 16 8mm fuchsia Swarovski bicone crystals
- 8 18mm × 10mm ruby in zoisite nuggets
- 268 $11/_0$ mint matte inside color seed beads
- 2 silver crimp tubes
- Sterling silver toggle clasp
- 16 sterling silver bead caps
- 8mm 18-gauge silver jump ring
- Crimp pliers
- 2 sets of chain-nose pliers
- Flush cutters
- Ruler
- Scissors
- Glue

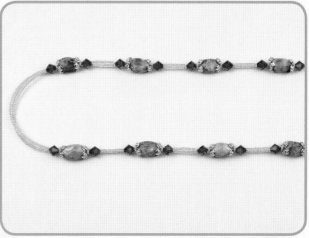

1 String a crimp tube, silver ball and one half of the toggle clasp onto both wire ends. Loop the wires back through the silver ball and crimp tube. Use crimp pliers to flatten and fold the crimp tube. Use flush cutters to cut the excess wire. String the following onto both wires: a crystal, a bead cap, a nugget, a bead cap and a crystal. Separate the wires and string 12 seed beads onto each wire. Repeat the beading pattern 2 more times.

2 String the following onto both wires: a crystal, a bead cap, a nugget, a bead cap and a crystal. Separate the wires and string 62 seed beads on each wire. Repeat the beading pattern from step 1 three times. String the following onto both wires: a crystal, a bead cap, a nugget, a bead cap, a crystal, a crimp tube, a silver ball and the other half of the toggle clasp. Loop the wires back through the silver ball and crimp tube. Pull the wire tight. Use the crimp pliers to flatten and fold the crimp tube. Use the flush cutters to cut the excess wire.

3 Make a dongsimgyeol maedeup with 2½" (6cm) loops. The finished loops will be approximately 1⅛" (3cm). Measure 1" (3cm) from the end of the maedeup and cut the excess cording. Glue the ends. Open the jump ring and slip it onto the top of the dongsimgyeol maedeup and the center two wires of the necklace. Close the jump ring.

"love" necklace

The Chinese characters on the charm in this necklace spell out "love." There are more than 80,000 Chinese characters, out of which about 3,500 cover 99 percent of what you would need to read Chinese. Korean children learn Chinese characters at school, but only a few hundred. Compare that to the twenty-six characters in our English language.

The Korean alphabet is called *Hangeul* and contains twenty-four characters. I have always found Asian lettering so beautiful. I discovered that Koreans feel the same way about English. They love to wear T-shirts and sweatshirts with English on them, and the words (if there are actual words) usually don't make any sense.

1 Attach the charm to the jump ring (see page 49). Thread the jump ring onto one cord. Fold the cord in half to find the center and move the charm to the center. Keep the charm near the fold and make two dorae maedeup. Thread both ends of the cord through the lampwork bead and make a dorae maedeup.

2 Take the second cord and make 3 wae dorae maedeup in the center.

3 Measure ½" (1cm) from the last wae dorae maedeup and make 3 additional wae dorae maedeup. Repeat once. Repeat this entire step on the other side of the original wae dorae maedeup. Center this cord parallel to the first cord.

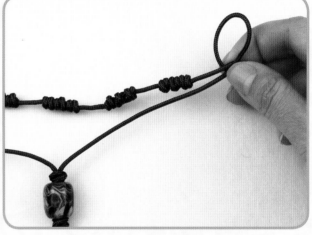

4 Measure 4" (10cm) from the dorae maedeup on the first cord and ½" (1cm) from the last wae dorae maedeup on the second cord. Loop the first cord over the second cord to make a dorae maedeup.

5 Make 3 dorae maedeup. Measure 1" (3cm) and make 2 dorae maedeup. Measure 3½" (9cm) and make 2 dorae maedeup. Finish with a garakji maedeup, tightening ½" (1cm) from the last dorae maedeup. Repeat steps 4–5 for the other side. Cut off the excess cording and glue the ends.

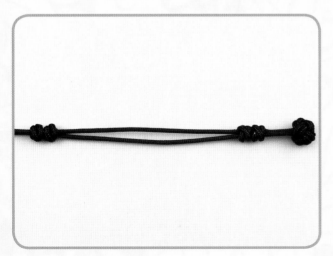

faceted crystal columns necklace

This necklace honors the Korean woman. I come from the United States, where throwing on a baseball cap, sweatshirt and jeans to run to the grocery store is the norm. Not so in Korea, where women regularly wear dress clothes to pick up groceries or to meet friends for coffee. Hair and makeup are always immaculate, too. Accessories are just as important. High heels are a must, and I frequently saw women dashing to a bus or the subway in them.

Dongdaemun Market in Seoul is the place to shop for clothing and accessories in Korea. There you will find thirty shopping malls that house more than 27,000 retail and wholesale shops. It was this incredible market that started my purse addiction.

Maedeup
- Dorae (pages 18–19)
- Nalgae (pages 22–23)
- Garakji (pages 28–30)

Materials
- 15' (4.5 meters) 1mm purple Korean cording, cut in half
- 7 20mm silver shade Swarovski faceted crystal columns
- Awl
- Ruler
- Scissors
- Glue

1 Thread a crystal to the center of one cord. Lay the second cord parallel to the first cord.

2 Make a dorae maedeup next to the crystal.

3 Make a total of 3 dorae maedeup on each side of the crystal.

4 Add a crystal and 3 dorae maedeup. Repeat one more time. Add a crystal and make 1 dorae maedeup. Repeat for the opposite side.

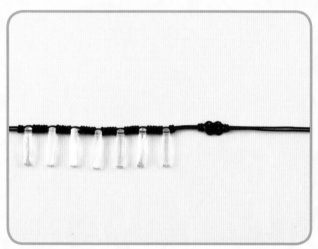

5 Measure ½" (1cm) from the dorae maedeup. Make a dorae maedeup, 2 nalgae maedeup and another dorae maedeup.

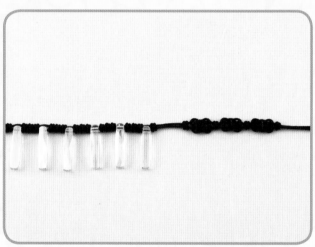

6 Repeat twice: 2 nalgae maedeup and a dorae maedeup.

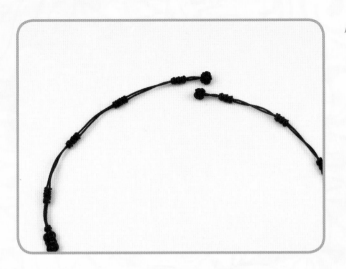

7 Measure ½" (1cm) from the dorae maedeup and make 3 dorae maedeup. Measure 1" (3cm) and make 3 dorae maedeup. Repeat 2 more times. Finish with a garakji maedeup, tightening ⅜" (1cm) from the last dorae maedeup. Repeat steps 5–7 for the opposite side. Cut off the excess cording and glue the ends.

Maedeup

- Dorae (pages 18–19)
- Saengjjok (pages 32–34)
- Hapjong (page 21)

Materials

- 7' (2.1 meters) 2mm variegated satin cording, cut in half
- 41mm × 33mm diamond tricolor copper pendant (Perle Nouveau)
- 11 $^6/_0$ green opaque frosted rainbow seed beads
- 2 large (approximately 3.5mm × 11mm × 5mm) fold-over crimp ends
- 2 5mm 20-gauge silver jump rings
- Sterling silver toggle clasp
- Awl
- Glue
- Toothpick
- Ruler
- Scissors
- 2 sets of chain-nose pliers

variegated satin cord necklace

I love the many colors of this variegated satin cording. They remind me of a typical Korean meal. There are always one or two types of *kimchi* (fermented and salted cabbage or radish with red pepper paste and garlic) and rice. Most meals are served with anywhere from six to ten, mostly vegetable, side dishes. Between meals, ramen (*ramyeon* in Korean) is the most popular snack food in Korea. Unlike ramen in the States, it is very spicy. I absolutely fell in love with Korean food during our stay, with only one exception—octopus.

1 Thread the pendant onto one cord. Fold the cord in half to find the center and move the pendant to the center. Keep the pendant near the fold and make a dorae maedeup, saengjjok maedeup and 2 more dorae maedeup.

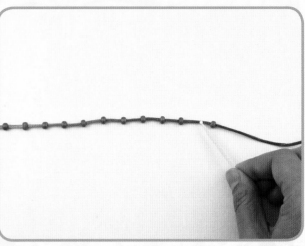

2 Take the second cord and thread a seed bead to the center of the cord. Glue it to the center. Add another bead, measure ½" (1cm) from the glued bead and glue the second bead. Add and glue a total of 5 beads to each side of the center bead.

3 Measure 4½" (11cm) from the dorae maedeup of the first cord and right after the last bead on the second cord. Make a dorae maedeup, 3 hapjong maedeup and another dorae maedeup. Repeat on the opposite side.

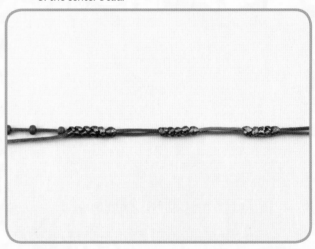

4 Measure 1" (3cm) from the last dorae maedeup and make a dorae maedeup, 3 hapjong maedeup and another dorae maedeup. Repeat. Repeat step 4 for the opposite side.

5 Attach the crimp ends, jump rings and toggle clasp to both ends (see pages 49–51).

A colorful Korean meal.

107

Maedeup

- Dorae (pages 18–19)
- Saengjjok (pages 32–34)
- Garakji (pages 28–30)

Materials

- 4' (1.2meters) 1.5mm chocolate brown Chinese cording
- 5 13mm soapstone beads
- Awl
- Ruler
- Scissors
- Glue

soapstone necklace

I found these soapstone beads at my local bead store in the States. The beads are really unique and caught my eye immediately. I bought them without having any idea of what I would do with them. They resided in a bead box and traveled to Korea with us. I used dorae and saengjjok maedeup to space the beads and finish the necklace. An alternative look is the use of consecutive dorae maedeup to complete the necklace after you finish adding all the soapstone beads. You must remember to increase the length of cording to accommodate the additional maedeup, which is why I like to plan out a project before I begin. Of course, you can almost always adjust something a bit during the construction. For example, you can switch to a fold-over crimp end and toggle clasp instead of a garakji maedeup, or a necklace can become a choker or a bracelet.

1 Thread a soapstone bead onto both cords. Fold the cords in half to find the center and move the bead to the center. Make a dorae maedeup on each side of the bead. Make a saengjjok maedeup and a dorae maedeup on each side.

2 Continue with the following on each side: soapstone bead, dorae maedeup, saengjjok maedeup and dorae maedeup. Thread a soapstone bead and make a dorae maedeup to finish each side.

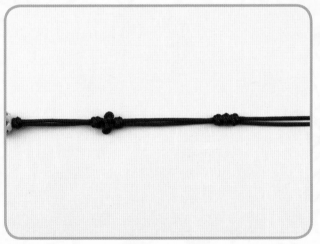

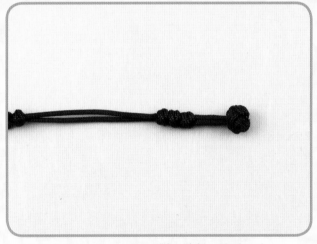

3 Measure 1½" (4cm) from the last maedeup and make a dorae maedeup, saengjjok maedeup and another dorae maedeup. Measure 2" (5cm) and make 3 dorae maedeup.

4 Make a garakji maedeup 1" (3cm) from the last dorae maedeup. When tightening the garakji maedeup, leave a ½" (1cm) space between the last dorae maedeup and the garakji maedeup.

5 Repeat steps 3–4 to complete the opposite side. Cut off the excess cording and glue the ends.

cherry blossom necklace

I never experienced the pleasure of cherry blossoms in the spring until our move to Korea. We lived about a mile from the Suwon Hwaseong Fortress, where I discovered cherry blossoms. Some of the walking paths at the fortress are lined with cherry trees, and as you walk you are shaded by their huge branches. In the spring, these paths become covered with cherry blossom petals, and it looks like it has snowed. Korean families and couples love to spend their free time enjoying the cherry blossoms. Everyone brings a camera to capture a special moment.

This project uses a sanjeongja maedeup, which is one of the more difficult maedeup to construct. You can substitute a saengjjok maedeup for each sanjeongja maedeup and it will still look beautiful.

Maedeup
- Dorae (pages 18–19)
- Sanjeongja (pages 38–40)
- Garakji (pages 28–30)

Materials
- 8' (2.4 meters) 1mm rose Korean cording
- 3 3¾" (9.5cm) (minimum 2.5mm hole) cherry blossom lampwork beads (Barbara Svetlick, see page 126)
- 18 3.5–3.7mm cream square beads
- Awl
- Ruler
- Scissors
- Glue

1 Thread a cherry blossom bead onto both cords. Fold the cords in half to find the center and move the bead to the center. Make 4 dorae maedeup on each side of the bead.

2 Make a sanjeongja maedeup on each side.

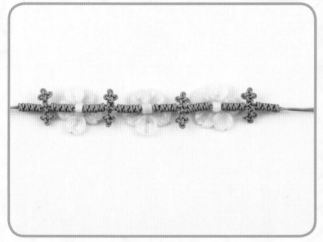

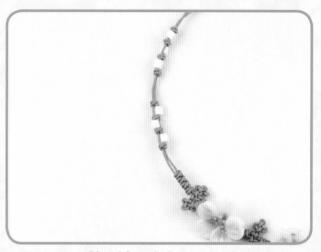

3 Continue with the following on each side: 4 dorae maedeup, cherry blossom bead, 4 dorae maedeup, sanjeongja maedeup and 4 dorae maedeup.

4 Measure ½" (1cm) from the last maedeup and make a dorae maedeup. String a square bead onto one cord and make a dorae maedeup. String a square bead on the opposite cord, followed by a dorae maedeup. Continue until you have 4 dorae maedeup and 3 square beads. Repeat step 4 two more times.

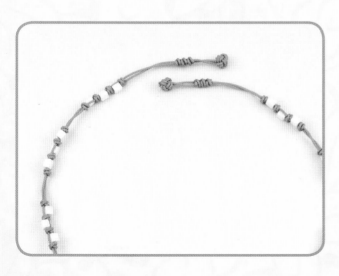

5 Measure 1" (3cm) from the last dorae maedeup and make 3 dorae maedeup. Make a garakji maedeup 1" (3cm) from the last dorae maedeup. When tightening the garakji maedeup, leave a ½" (1cm) space between the last dorae maedeup and the garakji maedeup. Repeat steps 4–5 to complete the opposite side. Cut off the excess cording and glue the ends.

Maedeup

- Saengjjok (pages 32–34)
- Dorae (pages 18–19)
- Garakji (pages 28–30)

Materials

- 10' (3 meters) 2mm olive green Korean cording, cut in half
- 3' (1m) 1mm gold metallic cording
- 5cm × 4.2cm green slices pencil pendant (Jennifer Maestre, see page 126)
- 7mm 24-gauge gold-plated jump ring
- Awl
- Loop turner
- Ruler
- Scissors
- Glue
- 2 sets of chain-nose pliers

saengjjok necklace

This project is unique in that you make two separate maedeup pieces that you attach with a jump ring when completed. This project also involves constructing consecutive saengjjok maedeup, which gives the maedeup a totally different look, much like a chain. When tightening each saengjjok maedeup, you will notice they form a natural curve, which makes the arrangement perfect for a necklace. I added the gold metallic cording to give the saengjjok maedeup a more sophisticated look.

Choose a larger pendant of at least 3" (8cm) to balance the width of the saengjjok maedeup. A smaller pendant would get lost in the piece. Silver cording works just as beautifully as the gold cording.

1 Make a saengjjok maedeup on one cord.

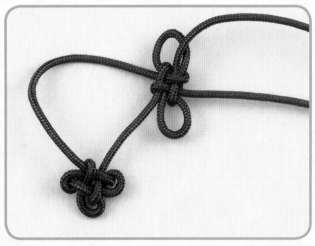

2 Make another saengjjok maedeup.

3 Tighten the second saengjjok maedeup up to the first. Make a total of 19 saengjjok maedeup. Repeat for the second cord. This will make the two halves of the necklace.

4 Beginning with one half of the necklace, put the loop turner through the center of the first saengjjok maedeup. Put the metallic cording into the loop turner. Pull the cording through the center, leaving a 1" (3cm) tail.

5 The center of the saengjjok is diamond-shaped. Place the loop turner through the top side of the diamond and put the metallic cording into the loop turner.

6 Pull the cording all the way through, making sure you don't pull out the tail. Place the loop turner into the next side and put the metallic cording into the loop turner.

7 Pull the cording until the new gold loop is the size of the green loop. Place the loop turner through the opposite side of the diamond and put the metallic cording into the loop turner.

8 Pull the cording until it is tight. Place the loop turner through the left side of the diamond and put the metallic cording into the loop turner.

9 Pull the cording until the new gold loop is the size of the green loop. Place the loop turner through the center from the opposite side you have been working on and put the metallic cording into the loop turner.

10 Pull the cording until it is tight. Place the loop turner through the center front and put the metallic cording into the loop turner. Pull the cording until tight. Repeat steps 5–10 until all the saengjjok maedeup are outlined in metallic thread. Cut the metallic thread, leaving a 1" (3cm) tail.

11 Repeat steps 4–10 for the second half of the necklace.

12 To bury the metallic cording ends, place the loop turner through the back on one of the lower sides of the diamond. Put the end in the loop turner. Pull until the cording is tight. Bury all four cording ends. Use scissors to cut off the excess cording.

13 Make a dorae maedeup with the green cording. Measure 1" (3cm) from the dorae maedeup and make 2 dorae maedeup. Make a garakji maedeup 1" (3cm) from the last dorae maedeup. When tightening the garakji maedeup, leave a ¾" (2cm) space between the last dorae maedeup and the garakji maedeup. Repeat for the opposite side of the necklace.

14 Cut off the excess cording and glue the ends. Open the jump ring (see page 49) and string one half of the necklace, the pendant and the other half of the necklace. Close the jump ring.

jeju island cloisonné necklace

Jeju Island is a South Korean island about an hour by plane from Seoul. It is a popular vacation and honeymoon destination for Koreans. The island is famous for its female divers who are usually between fifty and seventy-five years old. They boat out into the ocean and hold their breath as they dive up to 20 meters below the surface to gather clams, abalone and seaweed.

One of the crafts of Jeju Island is called *chilbo* (Korean cloisonné). I purchased the pendant used in this project from a shop on the island. We hired a taxi driver at a very reasonable rate to be our tour guide. He took us to all the main attractions, and we enjoyed sitting back and watching the scenery. It turned out that our driver also drove former President George H.W. Bush when he visited the island. Our driver even had a picture of the two of them to prove it.

Maedeup

- Dorae (pages 18–19)
- Nalgae (pages 22–23)
- Hapjong (page 21)
- Garakji (pages 28–30)

Materials

- 12' (3.6 meters) 1.5mm medium copper-colored Korean cording
- ⅞" × ¾" (23mm × 19mm) cloisonné pendant
- Awl
- Ruler
- Scissors
- Glue

1 Thread the pendant onto both cords. Fold the cording in half to find the center and move the pendant to the center. Make 3 dorae maedeup on each side of the pendant.

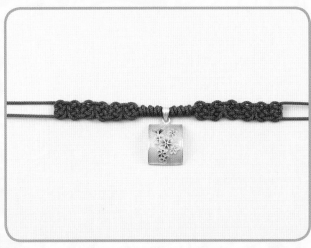

2 Make 6 nalgae maedeup on each side of the pendant.

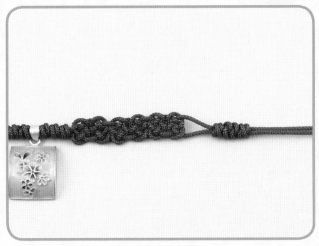

3 Measure ½" (1cm) from the last nalgae maedeup and make the following: dorae maedeup, 2 hapjong maedeup and another dorae maedeup.

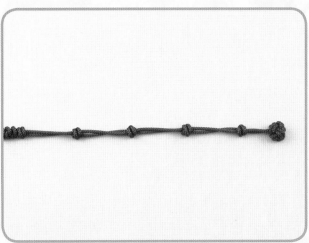

4 Measure 1" (3cm) from the last dorae maedeup and make a dorae maedeup. Repeat 3 more times. End with a garakji maedeup, tightening ½" (1cm) from the last dorae maedeup. Repeat steps 3–4 for the other side of the pendant. Cut off the excess cording and glue the ends.

The lava tubes of Jeju Island.

crystal pendant necklace

The cording used in this necklace reminds me of a type of Korean pottery called celadon (*cheong-ja* in Korean). Korean celadon has been around for centuries and can be recognized by its light green color. It takes more than ten steps to complete just one piece. Wood-burning kilns are still used to cure the pottery. I have a couple pieces I purchased during our stay in Korea, and I cherish them.

This necklace is a dramatic accessory for any outfit. It is a great conversation starter and always draws attention. I love to show off a pendant by using maedeup, and one of my favorite maedeup combinations (a saengjjok maedeup, a sanjeongja maedeup and another saengjjok maedeup) is used in this necklace.

Maedeup
- Dorae (pages 18–19)
- Saengjjok (pages 32–34)
- Sanjeongja (pages 38–40)
- Garakji (pages 28–30)

Materials
- 6 yds. (5.4 meters) 1.5mm medium forest green Korean cording, cut in half
- 1¼" (3.2cm) green crystal pendant
- Awl
- Ruler
- Scissors
- Glue

1 Thread one cord through the pendant. Fold the cord in half to find the center and move the pendant to the center. Make a dorae maedeup.

2 Make the following: saengjjok maedeup, sanjeongja maedeup, saengjjok maedeup and a dorae maedeup.

3 Take the second cord and center it alongside the first cord. Make a dorae maedeup.

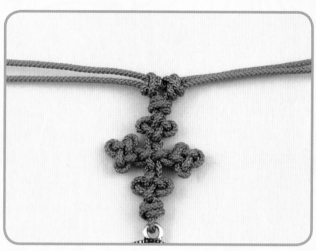

4 Make a second dorae maedeup on the opposite side of the center.

5 Continue with 3 more dorae maedeup on each side.

6 Measure 2½" (6cm) from the last dorae maedeup and make a dorae maedeup, saengjjok maedeup and another dorae maedeup. Repeat on the opposite side.

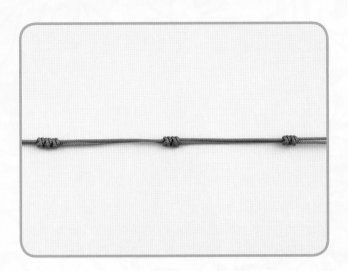

7 Measure 2½" (6cm) and make 3 dorae maedeup. Measure 2½" (6cm) and make 2 dorae maedeup twice. Make a garakji maedeup 1" (3cm) from the last dorae maedeup. When tightening the garakji maedeup, leave a ½" (1cm) space between the last dorae maedeup and the garakji maedeup. Repeat step 7 on the opposite side. Cut off the excess cording and glue the ends.

Hwaseong Fortress took two years to build—from 1794 to 1796 during the Joseon Dynasty (1392-1910). It was heavily damaged during the Japanese occupation (1910-1945) and the Korean War (1950-1953). It was rebuilt in the 1970's. This picture is one of the sentry posts.

conclusion

It was bittersweet that the final editing of this book coincided with our departure from South Korea. We had experienced the most amazing 21 months of our lives and it was ending. I was thrown into a panic of last-minute shopping for things I wanted before we left. As I hit all the major Seoul shopping markets, I realized that I wouldn't be able to take home what I wanted to the most: my Korean friends and the Korean culture that I had come to love so deeply.

I had a rough copy of the book printed out in a binder and I was showing it to one of my Korean friends, Jeff (Park Lang-Kyu). He was awestruck as he slowly turned each page and saw all that I had learned from his country. He told me that he was ashamed that he had never known the talent of his ancestors. It was a moment I will never forget.

What I hope you will take away from this book is a little knowledge of the Korean culture through maedeup and the discovery of a new craft that is as intriguing as it is beautiful. Maedeup and South Korea have forever changed my life, and I hope they will touch you in the same way.

gallery

Right: *Midnight in Seoul Necklace*
23" (58cm) necklace

Maedeup used: Dorae, saengjjok, garakji, seokssi, gyeonggari and ddalgi

Left: *Sherbet in Summer Necklace*
19" (48cm) necklace

Maedeup used: Yeonbong, dorae, saengjjok and garakji

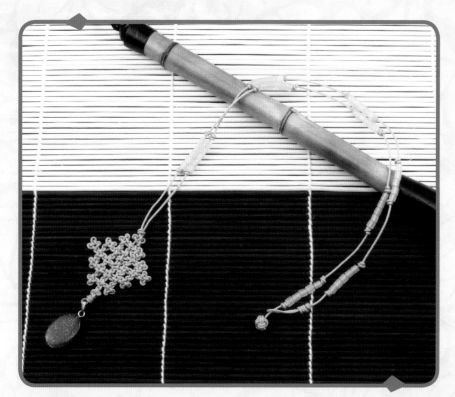

Left: *Goldstone Maedeup Necklace*
25" (63cm) necklace

Maedeup used: Wae dorae, dorae, saengjjok, garakji and seokssi

Right: *Chintz Necklace*
18" (46cm) necklace
Featuring lampwork beads by Krissy Beads
(www.krissybeads.com)

Maedeup used: Dorae, garakji and gajibangseok

resources

Barbara Svetlick
www.barbarasvetlick.com
Glass flower beads

Beacon Adhesives, Inc.
125 MacQuesten Parkway South
Mount Vernon, NY 10550
914-699-3405
www.beaconadhesives.com
Glue

Block Party Press
www.blockpartypress.etsy.com
blockpartypress@yahoo.com
Polymer clay sunflower pendant

Canterbury Keepsakes
Lezlie Belanger
www.cankeep.glasser.com
beads@cankeep.com
Lampwork beads

Jennifer Maestre
www.jennifermaestre.com
Pencil pendant

**KAS Lampwork Beads
and Silk Ribbons**
kasbeads@earthlink.net
Hand-dyed silk ribbons

Kim Miles
www.kimmiles.com
kim@kimmiles.com
Lampwork beads

Kreinik
1708 Gihon Road
Parkersburg, WV 26102
800-537-2166
www.kreinik.com
info@kreinik.com
Decorative threads

Nina Designs
P.O. Box 8127
Emeryville, CA 94662
800-336-6462
www.ninadesigns.com
nina@ninadesigns.com
Sterling silver beads and findings

Swarovski North America Limited
One Kenney Drive
Cranston, RI 02920
401-463-6400
www.create-your-style.com
Crystals

Toner Plastics
699 Silver Street
Agawam, MA 01001
413-789-1300
www.tonercrafts.com
sales@tonercrafts.com
FunWire

index

Explore the jewelry-making world with these other fine F+W Media books.

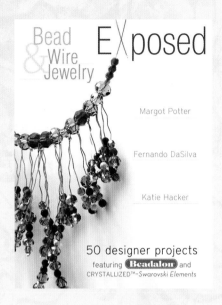

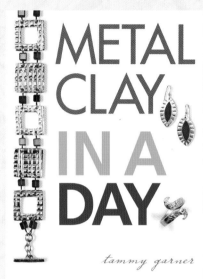

Bead & Wire Jewelry Exposed
Margot Potter, Katie Hacker and Fernando DaSilva

Bead & Wire Jewelry Exposed features over 50 high-fashion jewelry pieces made using techniques that reveal typically hidden components. Beading wire, cording, findings, tubing and chain take center stage in these clever designs. You'll learn to make shiny metallic wire or jump rings the focus of a design, and you'll see that a clasp can be decorative as well as functional. While the pieces may look complex, the techniques are simple enough for beginners—yet the designs are sophisticated enough for veteran jewelry crafters. Each of the three authors, Margot Potter, Katie Hacker and Fernando DaSilva, puts his or her spin on the exposed-element designs, so there's something for everyone.

ISBN-13: 978-1-60061-159-9
ISBN-10: 1-60061-159-1
Paperback • 144 pages • Z2508

Metal Clay in a Day
Tammy Garner

Metal Clay in a Day will show you how to make beautiful metal clay jewelry and components without breaking the bank! Learn how to cut, texturize and sculpt metal clay with inexpensive, easy-to-find equipment. Discover how to fire metal clay using a small butane torch, a great alternative to an expensive kiln. With a big dose of humor and a lot of practical know-how, author Tammy Garner will guide you through the basics of working with metal clay, as well as 25 fabulous metal clay projects, including earrings, necklaces, bracelets and more. If you're curious about metal clay, this is the introduction you've been looking for.

ISBN-13: 978-1-60061-079-0
ISBN-10: 1-60061-079-X
Paperback • 128 pages • Z1881

Mod Knots
Cathi Milligan

Revamping macramé for the next generation of crafters, Cathi Milligan's *Mod Knots* includes fashionable projects that showcase materials not typically associated with macramé, such as handspun yarn and wire, plus new twists on old favorites, like leather and waxed linen. Create 25 wearable projects—from a funky black leather cuff, to a summery bamboo-handle purse, to delicate wire chandelier earrings and a vibrant handspun yarn scarf.

ISBN-13: 978-1-60061-144-5
ISBN-10: 1-60061-144-3
Paperback • 128 pages • Z2382

These and other fine Krause titles are available at your local craft retailer, bookstore or online supplier, or visit our wesbite at **www.mycraftivitystore.com**.